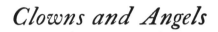

Clowns and Angels

BY THE SAME AUTHOR

❧

Books in English:

FROM CHARTERED LAND (Scott, New York)
ERNEST PSICHARI (Longmans, New York)

Books in French:

MATINES ET VERS (Figuière, Paris)
INTERVALLES (Cahiers des poètes, Bruxelles)
LA PURETÉ DANS L'ART (Editions de l'Arbre, Montréal)

In Preparation:

GRANDEUR DE LA PENSÉE FRANÇAISE (L'Arbre, Montréal)

Clowns and Angels

STUDIES IN
MODERN FRENCH LITERATURE

by
Wallace Fowlie

NEW YORK
COOPER SQUARE PUBLISHERS, INC.
1973

Originally published 1943 by Sheed and Ward, Inc.
Reprinted by permission of Sheed and Ward, Inc.
Published 1973 by Cooper Square Publishers, Inc.
59 Fourth Avenue, New York, New York 10003
International Standard Book Number 0-8154-0467-0
Library of Congress Catalog Card Number 72-93684

Printed in the United States of America

A
MARIE-LOUISE B.

qui s'appelle aujourd'hui
Soeur Brigitte
de l'ordre de Saint Dominique
à Montpellier
en France occupée

CONTENTS

Part III

THE POET'S CREATION

Part I
THE EXAMPLE OF FRANCE

THE EXAMPLE OF FRANCE

DURING PERIODS IN time such as the present one which we are passing through, when it is not exaggerated to say that the fate of great nations is in jeopardy, literature becomes a clearer manifestation of man's thought. Books which appeared obscure or difficult in periods of more relative peace reveal a poignant meaning to men who are forced by exterior circumstances and menaces to give their attention to what we might call the more profound problems of living.

The present day writers in France were not unaware in September 1939 of the events and conditions which had been preparing the European conflict. With very few exceptions, they are all convinced, even today in the silence which is imposed upon them, that France has a heritage to sustain, a mission to perform, and a future in which to hope. We in America, who are separated geographically from them, have never ceased being students of their art and their message. It is a commonplace to repeat that this contemporary age is transitional and therefore destined to produce no great, no lasting art. Great art does usually come from an historical synthesis, such as the Middle Ages which gave us a Dante, or the Renaissance which gave us a Shakespeare; but another great art, perhaps of a different kind, can emerge from a period of struggle such as our own. We feel that certain works which are to be mentioned in this book will eventually take their place beside the greatest works in French literature. The task we have set

3

ourselves is to indicate what can be indicated briefly concerning their peculiar quality and their contemporary meaning.

France has not been solely, since the time of Joan of Arc, the perpetual battlefield of western civilization; it has been also the crossroads of the two spirits or two values whose fusion has formed this particular civilization. Words are deceptive when we try to name these values, but for simplicity's sake, let us call them the classical spirit from the south and the gothic spirit from the north. Together, in that strange chemical commingling which we designate as French, they are in the paintings of Cézanne, in the music of Debussy, and in the poetry of Baudelaire. There are physical remains of Roman civilization in southern France: temples and arenas, aqueducts and roads. The plains and hills themselves of Provence have the clarity and simple lines we naturally ascribe to classic art. These are in the landscapes of Cézanne, a transcription of all that a southern sun can illuminate with that beauty which is peace. But there is also, on many of his canvases, the mistiness of what we might call a northern dream and a colder questioning. All that a personal soul can distort with independence and fervor is here in oils, lending to classical sobriety the more somber tones of a gothic night. And the chastened form of Debussy's work contains notes of strangely contrasting color. It is a design which reflects the clear reason of classicism but which also leaves freedom to the hesitancy of gothic irrationality. The modern Frenchman has inherited a capacity for lucid reasoning and precision as well as an insatiable need to investigate what torments man, or what he at least believes torments man.

The critical spirit has remained uppermost in the Frenchman's heritage. His language has nothing of the heavy ambiguousness of German and English. It is as clear and piercing as the light of a Cézanne sky or a Debussy piano piece. The organization of his art and that of his speech bears a remarkable effortlessness. Yet he faces all the contemporary problems, because he has always done this in every period of modern history, and brings to them his own particular reaction, his own particular solution. His art is critical and his criticism is composed with all the rigors of art. Man with his psychological and sociological dilemmas is the point on which converge both art and criticism, the first for his delectation and the second for his clarification. We are then considering here an art which is critical in its form and a criticism formed impeccably in its thought.

We begin with that form of writing which seems to be preeminently the modern form: the novel. Whether it be an imitation of life or a celebration of life or an essay on life, the novel can stretch its designs to encompass any end. Today, when all literary forms are enlarging their scope, the novel surpasses each in variety and flexibility.

I. *The Novel*

Ever since the time of Balzac, in the middle of the nineteenth century, there have been many efforts in France to make of the novel a vast complicated document. Man still remains, of course, the central figure in the novel, but the novelist's art deals more exclusively with the multiple forces that affect man. The novel then becomes the scene not of one drama but of many dramas, closely fitted into a complete structure of which it is often difficult to pick out the leading drama or the leading character. Characters tended, particularly in the early history of this genre, to become abstractions enrolled in the service of ideas. Thus Jean Valjean in *Les Misérables* typifies the victim of an ill-conceived justice, and Lantier in Zola's *Germinal* represents the victim of social injustice. Between Hugo and Zola there is a growing preoccupation with the historical or social moment in which the novel takes place. Society as a whole really becomes the hero. It is not until the work of Marcel Proust that the novel succeeds in painting a portion of society, that is, in presenting "evidence" and a sociological document, and, at the same time, in giving over the action of the novel to real characters. In this sense, Proust's *A la recherche du temps perdu* subsumed what had been done in the French novel up until the first World War. But in it he treated almost exclusively a disappearing social class, the aristocracy in Paris, with its particular idiosyncrasies and vices.

MALRAUX

The French novelist of today who shares with Jules Romains a considerable vogue in America is André Malraux. We shall see later in the chapter on *Les Hommes de Bonne Volonté*, how Romains uses a catastrophic scene, such as the first World War, when he comes to it chronologically, but Malraux is a writer who uses it almost exclusively. He seems to be at home in a great upheaval. His art is a chaos, particularly in his last book, but the element which gives it a profound unity is its passion. Persistent throughout all his work is the preoccupation with eternal things. Malraux has said that "the great blood-streaked manoeuvres of the world have begun." In his novel *La Condition Humaine*, he dealt with the Communist uprising in China. Malraux himself had played an important part in this revolt. In his brief novel *Le Temps du Mépris*, the scene takes place in a German concentration camp. And in the novel published in 1937, *Espoir*, it is the Spanish Civil War that is evoked—again a war in which Malraux himself served, as head of the air squadron for the Loyalist side.

At the end, Malraux's personal life will perhaps be a truer epic than his work. With the increasing gravity of the world situation, his work has become more and more that of a pointilliste painter, of a rapid note-taker and reporter. Malraux seems impatient in it, ill at ease with his writer's occupation which never equates in intensity the occupation of living and fighting. His song deals with man's suffering, with man's cruelty, with failure, with destiny, with man's longing for the absolute. These are all parts of Malraux's dominant theme: human dignity. Certain scenes of *La Condition Humaine* recall Dante's *Inferno*. Malraux's is the modern painting of a condemned humanity.

Both the documentary novel of Jules Romains and the tragic-heroic novels of André Malraux describe the critical "impasses" of our age. But "good will" is in the title of one and "hope" is in the title of the other. Their meaning, more profound than perhaps they themselves realized, is today transparent.

II. *The Theatre*

The theatre in France recently has in nowise equalled the novel in fecundity. It is a more difficult genre to work in, and the public is less willing to accept experimentation when they pay for it of an evening. Yet there are a few isolated efforts in dramatic literature which seem highly significant and which, for our purposes, illustrate even better than the novel does, the rehabilitation of certain constant themes and values in French culture.

GIRAUDOUX

Jean Giraudoux is not solely a dramatist; his plays represent a greater synthesis of his thought than do his novels. In his plays he has set forth more succinctly than in his other writings his best criticism. Here we are using criticism in its highest sense—not as a listing of errors on one side and a listing of reforms on the other but as a metaphysical plunge into the past for the light of the future, as a rediscovery of man's permanent heritage and dignity.

At the beginning of this war no writer in France had warmer admirers or colder adversaries than Giraudoux. His language is an ever-present proof that everything can be resaid differently. He has the fecund imagination of a poet who writes in prose—no poet would or could permit himself Giraudoux's abundance of baroque images. But Giraudoux is not only a stylist in preciosity; he has in his nature and exploits in his writings all the traits of a typical Frenchman: bourgeois traits and rationalistic ones; the satire of Paris and the tenderness of the provinces. Again, it is due to this strange mixture of poetry that is at once malicious and aerial that we can follow this art which is never without psychology and this psychology which is never without art. Giraudoux appears almost the representative French writer today. His zone is the temperate one; his art is the closest to Cézanne's and Debussy's.

Giraudoux sees as deeply into the present as Romains and Malraux, but his work has achieved the luminous equilibrium of more faith than theirs. It may seem at first a work ridiculously clear and simple, but one has to look for a long time into clear waters in order to see their depths.

The comedies of Molière and the fables of La Fontaine deceive also by the clarity of their form.

In most of his plays Giraudoux resurrects an ancient story, usually Greek: *Amphitryon 38, La Guerre de Troie n'aura pas lieu, Electre*. This last was performed in 1937. In the light of contemporary events *Electre* speaks a fuller message than the other plays of Giraudoux. It is a play which deals with two seemingly contradictory themes: purity and revolution. Electra is the pure one, the virgin who demands justice and who will not hesitate to throw a city into revolution in order that justice may be achieved. Through this Greek theme Giraudoux has attained a striking modernity. Electra symbolizes not only a type in history but also a moment in history. Humanity may harbor within itself for a long time ingredients of disaster and crime, but usually at the end there will arise a great character: an Electra or a Joan of Arc, who will insist that the wrong be righted, that humanity be purged. The *Electre* of Giraudoux has that nobility which comes from a great decision and that modesty which seems an element of classical art.

In the final scene of the play, the palace burns and Electra stands before it knowing that nothing remains for her except her conscience and justice. A woman beside her asks what people call that thing which rises with the day after all has been demolished and burned. Electra turns to a beggar for the answer. His words close the play as he says: "Cela a un très beau nom. Cela s'appelle l'aurore."

Cocteau

Despite the legend which has masked him for some years, Jean Cocteau appears now as one of the few writers of our time who have understood the meaning of tragedy.

While in the theatre of Cocteau there is in evidence a very cruel fatality and determinism, in his critical writings and poetry there is an aphoristic expression and jumbling of terms which make hazardous any assurance about his dramatic or literary theory. The lesson of equilibrium which Cocteau refers to so constantly in *Le Rappel à l'Ordre* is the lesson he learned at the Cirque Médrano with Picasso,[1] Apollinaire, and Max Jacob. It seems first to have been a lesson of simplicity in formal structure. But more than that, it appears now to have been a lesson of simplicity in a spiritual sense: the meaning of the creative process, the value of a work of art as contrasted with the value of man, the whole psychological and religious problem of "man the artist," which has become for our century the most tenacious of literary themes.

Two phrases, found in Cocteau's celebrated letter to Jacques Maritain, will be the basis for our discussion of Cocteau's tragedies. The first is a literary comment, a call to arms of the artist of about 1920. "Il s'agissait de déniaiser quelques genres." That is, Cocteau felt it incumbent upon himself to make less stupid some literary genres, among which he lists tragedy. And the second phrase is one in which he defines men as being gawky peasants from heaven, "lourdauds du ciel que nous sommes."

The barest tragedies of Cocteau, those in which he least depends on melodramatic magic, are the ones which represent his operations on Greek tragedies. In *Antigone*, for example, he gives a rapid reduced picture of Sophocles. Much is lost perhaps in the cutting, but something also is gained: a tempo which is that of our age and a clarity of action which is a lesson for our age. Cocteau has described himself as being above the Greek text and looking down at it as though from an airplane. He has brought out new colors for us to see in it, new blocks and angles, but he has above all composed a work which unfolds in time with the absolute, in accordance with the function of the absolute.

This new order, discovered for an ancient structure, was already a creative act for Cocteau, but his *Machine Infernale* shows his fullest development in handling a Greek theme. Although the new Oedipe slightly resembles a gigolo who, paradoxically, has preserved his chastity, he feels all the awkwardnesses of living which are implied in Cocteau's definition that man is an impotent angel exiled from heaven. The light of the sun which Antigone had sung of is now replaced by a dream world in which the devil reigns. Tirésias, in both plays, is the priest who understands all the legends without always understanding reality. The chorus in *Antigone* and Tirésias in *La Machine Infernale* speak for the poet whose constant warning seems to be that man has no proportion with nature.

Oedipus is the proud hero who is bent upon deceiving the stars and at the same time a man sufficiently great for Destiny to heed. For Jocasta the queen, he is always the child to be caressed, and for Tirésias the priest, he is the one inexplicable mystery in the realm. Cocteau has maintained in Oedipus the dual focus of magnitude and frailty. As did his Antigone, his Oedipus represents both a sublime individual and a self-annihilated fate.

Thus, in the work of Cocteau, tragedy emerges in its purest state, with its fullest meaning. It is the dual vision of grandeur and frailty, the sole vision which will permit the spectator to be moved by disaster and to accept it in art. It is, in a way, a new incarnation of man whom Pope defines as "the Glory, Jest and Riddle of the World."

In his last two plays, *Les Chevaliers de la Table Ronde* of 1937 and *Les Parents Terribles* of 1938, Cocteau seems to have broken off with Greece. He continues, however, to be as oracular in these dramas as he was in his Greek tragedies. *Les Chevaliers de la Table Ronde* has little mediaeval exactitude. Cocteau explains in a preface how the story was dreamt by him and then composed as a play two years after the dream. He further explains that it is only by chance that his play is moral. It does appear to us to be profoundly Christian in tone, and even faintly resembles Shakespeare in its confusion and complication. Galahad is Cocteau's pure hero who disintoxicates a castle drugged with vice and falseness. At the end of the play Truth is reinstalled in the Castle of Camelot by means of murder and Arthur does not hesitate to say, "J'aime mieux de vrais morts qu'une fausse vie." As in Cocteau's *Antigone*, where the chorus is recited by a single voice echoing the struggle of the One against the Many, so in *Les Chevaliers de la Table Ronde*, Ginifer, the principal character, who is the demon controlled by Merlin, enters some of the true characters only to make them false. The struggle of man with himself remains the same. It is somewhat more mediaeval in the sense that it is more of a dance, or more of a supernatural nightmare.

A rapid examination of *Les Parents Terribles* might lead one to see in it an old fashioned melodrama. It is much more. In addition to being one of the most skillfully constructed plays of Cocteau, it is one of the most poignant, in a tragic sense. The theme of "order," apparent in all of Cocteau's writings, is here more dominant than ever. The character Léo is a new Electra who has the passion for establishing order everywhere. Yvonne, the mother, is the tragic heroine who refuses to see herself and who therefore succumbs to the domination of disorder. It is a play about the triumph of order and, as always in Cocteau, order is that state which is attained after a clear understanding of oneself. As Maritain has pointed out, Cocteau is profoundly Thomistic. From the reading of this single play, *Les Parents Terribles*, one realizes that the poet is saying: Evil is blindness; evil results from the willful refusal to *see*.

These last two plays of Cocteau are not Greek, therefore, in any obvious way. But they are Greek in their depiction of tragedy as being the working out of laws, irrespective of whether they be right or wrong.

The portrayal of emotion in any romantic sense is practically absent from the work of Cocteau. There are many moments in his plays, filled by entire scenes, when his writing has that elegance of diction which may easily be called classical. "J'apprendrai que l'art est religieux," he wrote some years ago in his letter to Maritain. Cocteau has learned this lesson better than any other dramatist of our age. The almost childlike seriousness of his plays, their tension, and above all, perhaps, their implacable logic, mark them as feats in artistic strategy. At times they appear almost akin to some primitive witchcraft. His film, *Le Sang d'un Poète*, is a mixture of abstraction and imagery of such subtlety that it is also a metaphysical explanation of the modern artist. The purification of the senses and their renewal, needed by the modern artist:—Antigone descending to her tomb and Oedipus inflicting blindness upon himself —seems to have been the point of departure in ideas for Cocteau. The aesthetics of the tight-rope may be interpreted as being the aesthetics of the new liberty. Cocteau is as jealous of liberty as are the characters in his plays. And he is tragic in the same sense that Galahad is tragic—Galahad, who is able to show the Grail to others but who is unable to see it himself.

In his dual rôle of author and producer, Cocteau has participated both in the fabrication of his text and the technique of its projection in the theatre. I use advisedly the verb "participate," because Cocteau has appropriated in his credo a part of the conviction of his surrealist friends when he assigns to the creative process a certain amount of automatism. One is amazed at the number of deep-sea divers who appear in his early poetry and at the number of angels suspended over his later work. "Nous abritons un ange, que nous choquons sans cesse. Nous devons être gardiens de cet ange." The Greek tragedy of fate where the hero is blinded by an all-powerful force crushing him has become a very natural concept to this modern hero who is content with composing a work and then abandoning it to its own fate and who prefers the obscurity which may come from a simple denuded work of art to the falseness which disfigures a verbose overstuffed one.

There is a seeming facility in Cocteau's text which may cause it for some time to be scorned by the public. (The public is always hostile to an art at once simple and profound.) But the tragedy of his exercises is precisely this same tragedy: that of people who cannot see the world because it is too simple and luminous to be seen.

III. *Poetry*

The kind of criticism and observation which appears in the tragedies of Cocteau has been prevalent also among the poets. Jean Cocteau is a lyric poet as well as a dramatist, and he has been a guide for poets and critics of this last generation. The essays he wrote during the eight years which followed the first World War and which are published under the title *Le Rappel à l'Ordre* are a landmark in the development of French criticism. It is true that they are infinitely difficult, but that is because they try to define and analyze the creating intellect of the artist. The obscurity of the modern poetical form was an established fact. But the poets themselves had not called their verses "obscure." They were using the word "pure." It is possible to consider their attempts at creating "pure poetry" comparable to the words of the "pure" Electra of Giraudoux and the "pure" Galahad of Cocteau, all intent upon a cataclysmic renovation. In order to attain this new purity, the poets quite deliberately entered upon a régime of abstraction. Poetry became a rendez-vous for philosophy and song. The poetic conscience has never been more alive than it is today.

Since the poetry of Baudelaire, French poetry has been engaged in the exploration of new domains, but they are new domains in terms of romantic poetry not in terms of an earlier period such as the Renaissance or the classical age. Our age has simply rediscovered that French poetry is the daughter of abstraction and that its greatness, even its "lyrical" greatness, lies in its power to evoke all emotions and all thoughts with studied form and with images stripped of facile music. The debate on "pure poetry," the manifesto of surrealism, the essays of Cocteau, and the verse of Mallarmé and Valéry all testify not to some special and extraordinary manifestation of French art but to a central one. The modern French poets have simply discovered in their heritage and in their language the principles with which they have formulated their so-called new art.

The modern movement in poetry represents, then, not

obscurity but renovation, not "artiness" but a reawakening of traditional art. Values have not been discarded but have been reversed. In a word, the new art represents a defeat of all that was superficial and philosophically unsound in romanticism. In France the stars of the four great romantics are sinking: Lamartine, Hugo, Musset, Vigny. And in their place new and old ones are rising: Maurice Scève, Gérard de Nerval, Paul Valéry.

IV. *Gide*

We have seen that in the novels of Romains and Malraux and in the plays of Giraudoux and Cocteau the writer is principally concerned with man himself, with man in society as Romains shows him, with man versus society as Malraux shows him. The writings of poets have limited this general study of man to a study of the artist and to an analysis of the artistic work. Some prose writers also have been confronting this problem, particularly those who have recently published their personal journals. The French have a predilection for personal journals, and quaintly enough, a habit of publishing them during their own lifetime. André Gide published in 1939 his journal in one volume of 1,300 pages, covering fifty years of his life, the years between 1889 and 1939.

In Gide's work are synthesized all the trends and perceptions and movements which we have been enumerating. When we discussed the French writer as being a particular combination of artist and critic, it was Gide who appeared to us as the best contemporary example. We almost made this statement about Giraudoux, but in Gide's work there is none of Giraudoux's rhetorical excesses. At the source of each of his many books there is a personal moral issue, but he has raised it in each case to a higher, more universal application. How has he done this? By means of the patient discipline which true art requires. The "tone" of his books is the "tone" of classical art. He is the classicist because he is the artist who is willing to prepare himself for the work, who is willing to wait. His art confronts all the various problems of man: man as a solitary being, man as a social being, man as a creature of God; but his art refuses to treat any one of these problems tearfully. All the questions about life are maintained in art, according to Gide, but they exist there not so much in order to reveal the thought of the artist as to stir the thought of the reader. Gide doesn't believe that a novelist can say everything about a character. There should be a kind of free space around every work which will guarantee the dignity of each character and consecrate, so to speak, the mystery of each character.

The journal form of writing which Gide has often used in his novels and stories, as well as in his personal journals, is a genre eminently suitable to his sincerity. The journal is a kind of searching, comparable in music to the form of the fugue. No theme is ever lost. Every idea and every emotion recur, but altered by their new context. Every theme acquires a new force because of the construction of the past and its clearer vision of the future. Gide is the artist of human "becoming." He is the artist who believes that every hour in a man's life will count. Gide is able to separate himself from each character in his books in order to see what is superior to himself.

We can see here the courageous effort of contemporary art as contrasted with the art of the first half of the nineteenth century. The ego of the artist is no longer content with the contemplation of its own imperfections. It has been emancipated for a new kind of purity. And this is a purity which, I believe, is found only in art. Here we touch on a curious paradox: because in art the personality that is affirmed is the personality that has ceased living. The artist as a man continues to change, continues to become. His art is the picture of some arrested moments in his life.

The fugue is a form of music which is carefully constructed and yet it is never a form which sacrifices vision for explanation. In contemporary French literature we have examples of construction which, in terms of art, is that love for form, and this construction is applied to themes which are the eternal ones of man as man, and man as artist. The greatest works of our time testify to these standards. They are in the *Journal* of André Gide where the artist is in the humbled position of worker and seeker. They are in the paintings of Cézanne which, lineless in order to attain a greater purity, are solely constructions in color.

V. *France*

It is difficult to contemplate the fate of France today with any feeling other than that of horror and dismay. After serving the world as a kind of mistress of freedom, she is now virtually a slave, silenced and bound to a discipline which is contrary to all her traditions. But the spiritual strength of the French nation has not been weakened. It is covered and hidden very deeply in the warm and collected consciousness of the French people. There it will remain, but not inactive. It will not cease developing in purity and force.

The tragedy of France is not only that of a great nation of art and culture and freedom, but it is the tragedy of the country which had shown the greatest promises today of reinvigorating Christianity and making it count in the lives of its people. Throughout the history of France, her comprehension of Catholicism has been special and profound. It seems, moreover, that this religious vitality has been a major reason for the place which France has occupied in the growth of western civilization. Despite an anti-clerical France and despite an enlightened France (with all the modern meaning which adheres to the word "enlightened"), it seems to have been the chosen country for the new testing of Christian principles, the country whose mission seems to be the integration of Christian truth in all the country's activities. France represents precisely this experiment in civilization: ten centuries of Christianity and ten centuries of intellectual freedom during which the thought of man was constantly checking the validity and power of these religious principles. The experiment has turned out in favor of Christianity. France maintains her faith after having submitted it to all manner of tests and vicissitudes.

The war of 1914–18, despite economic betrayals, did cause to emerge in France a Christian kind of heroism in the figures of such men as Ernest Psichari and Charles Péguy. The example of their heroism did not die out with the war but has continued for twenty years and has never ceased to strengthen Christian convictions. Psichari died at the beginning of the war, after writing his brilliant defense of military heroism when it is crowned with Christian heroism. The mark of the Catholic Faith was on him, and his life gesture was its recognition. Péguy was also killed at the beginning of the war after discovering the meaning of socialism when it is enriched by Christian charity. His was the discipline of a man and a soldier who faces a supernatural end. The action of these two writers was felt in the war which was a prelude to the present crisis, and their heroism was a reaffirmation of the spiritual heritage which had formed their country.

A positive work of social reconstruction has been going on in France for these past twenty years. In addition to the economic readjustment, there has been the effort to reintegrate religious attitudes in social problems. It is precisely on this point that France seems to be the foremost country (and has indeed been since the Renaissance), that is, the country where one problem is never isolated from other problems. France has not denied the manifold implications of any one social problem for the other domains of religion, morals, politics. The French mind has been prepared by the cultural history of France to recognize the bonds which tie a single human being simultaneously to various loyalties. The Jocist movement (*Jeunesse Ouvrière Chrétienne*), which had reached before the war broke out in 1939 a marked period of strength, represents in French socialism that search for clear definition and reasonable demands by the working classes, while maintaining at the same time the firm determination to uphold the purest of Christian traditions. The Jocists refused to oppose in their form of socialism the terms "justice" and "charity" (as world socialism had been doing), but sought to conciliate them by means of a total understanding of the terms in the light of Christian theology.

Philosophically and practically, this work of Christian socialism has been promoted and aided by some of the best minds of contemporary France. In the Church itself, Cardinal Verdier of Paris and Father Ducattillon of the

Dominican Order are eminent examples of priests who have taken to heart the difficult problems of social reconstruction and who have both preached and written lessons of direction. François Mauriac and Jacques Maritain are two examples of writers who have turned their art and philosophy to the service of social enlightenment and exploration. Many others could be mentioned with these four names who, with conviction, piety, boldness, and learning, have brought their various specializations to bear on the pressing social issues of Christendom. Even the work of a painter like Rouault and of a poet like Claudel plays its part in this renewed vision of human destiny. In each case, the Frenchman's service to his particular work or art is made all the greater by his service to humanity.

Of these men, one has died; some have remained in France; and others are here in America. They, like the people of the country they have served, await the liberation —the end of the war—in order to resume their confrontation of social problems. France will again become the country preeminently capable of solving our difficulties because she continues to produce men who seek to understand first themselves as individuals, then to understand themselves as members of an immediate community, of a nation, and of the world. Such men are fully aware that the profoundest principles are involved even in the establishment of a just economic system.

The mission of France has been (and will continue to be after the present world crisis has passed) to teach the meaning of the Christian principles of charity and justice. Pascal in the seventeenth century and Cardinal Verdier of our age both taught that charity is a theological virtue which involves the love of God and the love of one's neighbor.

Part II

THE CONTEMPORARY HERO

ANDRE GIDE:
The Non-Catholic Tradition

I

THE LITERARY PORTRAIT of André Gide has already been made many times and, with few exceptions, he has always failed to recognize himself in it. The contradictions in his life and work make false and even ridiculous a simplified critical effort to categorize him, to assign him to some limited sphere or to tag him with some label. He is an artist, an artist in words. And he appears to us as one of the most massive. One of those whose work will attract all critics, whose work will seem to expound many creeds and support opposing theories. If Gide seems to appear in one book an amoralist, in the next book he will appear a rigorous, soul-searching moralist. If some pages make him out an unbeliever, other pages reveal a mind saturated with the Gospels and a fervent disciple of the words of Christ. The dangerous word "freedom" can appear in his writings in a hedonistic garb and in a communistic garb. The very form of his work, also, has surprises which seem to verge on contradictions. We find side by side the reduced, sober story of *La Porte Etroite* with few characters, few settings, and one theme; the richly populated, intricately assembled *Faux-Monnayeurs*; the lyric prose of *Amyntas* with its song of individualism and sensory experience; the critical book on Dostoievsky; the ironic "sotie" on the badly chained

Prometheus. Which is the central book in this long work? Which man is Gide in this long list of heroes? These are useless questions in the case of Gide. He himself is the subject of all his books, but all of them together do not compose a picture of himself which is totally true.

The complexity of Gide's mind seems to come from his very particular kind of sincerity. His background was moralistic and puritanical. More than any other vice, the Protestant hates the vice of falsehood. All his life Gide has been repulsed and horrified with lying when he encountered it. He has often accused Catholicism of not loving truth enough and of permitting accommodations with truth. Although his Catholic friends often told him he was confusing truth with God and forgetting that truth is not God but an attribute of God, he persisted in his distrust of what he considered subterfuge and deceit.

The effect of a serious puritanical home on a child's nature which is essentially tender, affectionate, and sentimental has been, in more cases than one, to produce a painful adolescence and a maturity whose major happiness consisted in a self-expression in some artistic medium. Gide realized in very early manhood that he had enough tearfulness in his soul to irrigate thirty books. This was his natural heritage. From his education—that is, from his early education at home—he acquired the habit of self-discipline and honesty. The desire for instruction in a nature like Gide's, for the annual making-over of oneself, for that puritanical revival, is capable of assuming the magnitude of a temptation. No critic seems to realize that when Gide, as a young writer, went to Africa in order to "give himself up to life" and thereby appeared to renounce conventional standards and bourgeois living, he was submitting himself to a severe discipline. It isn't easy for a puritan to discover and test out his naïve desires. To act in accordance with one's most instinctive desires, when one is not only a puritan but a "sincere" puritan as well, requires both resoluteness and perspicacity.

The African discipline of this puritan helped to make him into a French artist. There in Africa he came upon the belief that everything in life, every experience, could mean something to him. The African experiment, which I firmly believe was not a denial of all that by which Gide had lived previously but rather a logical continuation of self-instruction and self-analysis, taught him that everything in the universe must be reexamined and requestioned each day. There is no placidity for the sincere man, no established truth which will resist the distortion of time and human infidelity. The man who is thus willing to rediscover everything each morning of his life never ceases to work upon himself. Likewise he will never admit that anything can harm him; rather, everything can serve him in some way. He will turn every experience into some form of personal profit.

Gide's attitude toward religion is a clear illustration of his regimen of life. He found Catholicism inadmissible. He found Protestantism intolerable. And yet he felt himself to be profoundly Christian. Both branches of the Christian Church had, he believed, turned against Christ. For the Catholic side, Saint Paul had helped to define theological dogmas in an inflexible system or required beliefs. And for the Protestant side, Calvin, in an equally inflexible way, had helped to devise the moral pattern of human behavior. Saint Paul and Calvin are two screens which conceal the pure lesson of the Messiah. Also on the religious plane,

Gide has always shown a distrust, and even hate, of mysticism, because the domain of mysticism is beyond reason and defies reason. At moments of deep feeling on this subject, he could even consider as his personal enemies those philosophers, such as Plotinus, who seek to turn man away from life.

It has not been pointed out, I believe, that this very anguish of Gide over what he feels to be the errors of religion and mysticism, is of a quasi-mystical order itself. In him cohabit extremes. A habit of extreme discipline and an extreme need for constantly fresh material to be disciplined. "Je ne suis jamais; je deviens," he wrote in his journal.

The effort to be sincere provoked a relentless reexamining and reevaluating of persons, ideas, beliefs, works of art, sensations. This effort is one of the major explanations of his literary work. It is the major explanation of why happiness for Gide is not in comfort or in quietude but in what he calls ardor. In effort itself he finds a well-nigh perfect satisfaction. The unifying characteristic of Gide is his sincerity. But perhaps the quest for truth during a lifetime, when the quest itself is the real stimulation, weakens any profound desire to attain the truth. To attain truth by believing in it implies the submerging of oneself in it. This, Gide has not done.

II

Any attempt to study the relationships between Gide and his period will reveal the same quality of contradiction we have seen in his personal character. Morals, aesthetics, sociology, politics are themes which mingle or appear isolated in his work, and they represent the leading contemporary themes. Gide is one of those artists who apprehend the problem of the moment but who use it in such a way as to irritate the public which understands the problem in another way.

Gide has never founded a school. That would be contrary to all his belief and practice. But there is surely no writer in France who has had more influence on writers than he. Yet he has never recognized himself in them. What his mind attaches to is the future book. Only the unfinished book excites passion in him. It is justifiable to say that he has never sought, in any obvious way, to be of his period. (This, indeed, would affect his sincerity and his need for change.) He has actually sought to exceed his period, to overflow his period, to be the pioneer for a new period. His very change from a morality of privation (his first morality) to a morality of expansion forced him into the rôle of innovator.

"Except a man be born again" is one of his favorite sentences from the New Testament. It has served him as a kind of basic formula for the pattern of his life. This pattern has, in a sense, led Gide to a detachment from his century, but a detachment which, according to his thought, will prevent infidelity to his century and will help prepare a new kind of century. "Except a man be born again" is a text which means to Gide the writer that for each new book of his a new public will have to be won over. It is true that, except for the publication of his journal in 1939, none of his books had an immediate commercial success. In fact, three of his books, which today seem among his most important, *Paludes*, *Les Nourritures Terrestres*, and *Les Caves du Vatican*, were failures when they first appeared. It took ten years for the publishers of *Les Nourritures*

Terrestres to sell the first edition of five hundred copies. For Gide, each book was the evaluation of some uncertainty, and for his public it was in most cases the mysterious application of some theory which seemed unwholesome. But Gide believed that his books were not destined to reveal his own thought to the reader but rather to reveal the reader's thought to himself. "Jette ce livre—et sors. Je voudrais qu'il t'eût donné le désir de sortir—sortir de n'importe où, de ta ville, de ta famille, de ta chambre, de ta pensée."

Today, in retrospect, it is quite possible to see that there did exist a kind of relationship between Gide and his period, a spiritual affinity between the work and the moment of its creation. Each book now seems to illustrate a specific theme and bear a relation to the time of its publication. His first book, *André Walter*, is a book of the nineties, a work of symbolism and decadence, the prose-poetry written by a youth of twenty during a self-imposed exile on the Lac d'Annecy, a book of warm eloquent dedications sent to the great men of the time. *La Porte Etroite* is Gide's verdict on that form of love between man and woman which touches on mysticism. Alissa is one of his most moving characters and is, without any question, a faithful portrait of his wife. It was written in that easy pre-war period around 1908 when the world seemed in a prosperous peace and when a Frenchman could encourage his eternal interest in the psychology of love and religion. *Les Faux-Monnayeurs* appeared in the twenties, that period between two wars, and it deals with themes which that period pursued too exclusively: psychologism, child delinquency, the place of the artist in society.

III

The sincerity of Gide as a man, which forced him to examine each idea he came upon and to test for himself the validity of each theory, is a kind of heroism. And the sincerity of Gide as a writer, which made each book at the time of its composition an indispensable book for Gide to write, is also a kind of heroism. Let us examine one of his stories in order to consider more closely one of his heroes and the particular kind of heroism he represents in comparison with the heroism of a classical hero.

At the turn of the century Gide published his short novel or "récit," *L'Immoraliste*, which is an illustration and precision of his earlier *Nourritures Terrestres*. The lyricism of the *Nourritures* is in *L'Immoraliste* converted into a story; the de-personalized Nathanael, who had undergone the African régime of "ferveur," becomes the hero Michel, who in his turn is destined to discover in Africa a new code of morals. Like Hamlet's, Michel's life has been occupied with study; like Hamlet, Michel accepts the love of a woman without realizing that this love should be welcomed and reciprocated—that it is a love anxious to bestow itself and not live eternally in expectation. Soon in the story, Michel comes upon the momentous discovery of his illness. He hears it dictate to him a new way of life, as the words of the ghost reveal a new vocation to the lonely prince before he has really known love. Illness makes Michel realize the meaning of health, which he will not be long in equating with life. Whereas Hamlet needs to commit a deed in order to liberate his soul for love, Michel's liberation of his body from illness does not point toward any subsequent action. Gide's work does not celebrate liberation for any specific purpose; it simply celebrates liberation as a complete experience.

Gide's immoralist undertakes a search which is comparable to Proust's search backward in time; but it is a search for the key of the present. Michel, like all the heroes of Gide, is determined to understand his own nature by willfully removing his masks of habit, convention, conscience. To illustrate this, at one point in the text of *L'Immoraliste*, Gide employs the very beautiful metaphor of palimpsests. Michel compares his life to a palimpsest and wants to read the oldest text of himself; that is, the most authentic. In order to do this, he will have to efface all the more recent texts, which are false compared with the primitive one. The action of the story seems to be precisely this: to discover the primitive desires of the hero which still remain, no matter how disguised and changed. The accomplishment of these desires does not take place in the work. Michel approaches their very nomenclature with the foreboding of a man caught in the rigors of a moralistic system.

The character Ménalque in *L'Immoraliste*, who appears very briefly, speaks bolder words than those of Michel. The hero in most of Gide's books is portrayed during the period of his life which precedes any possible accomplishment. It is usually a secondary character, like Ménalque, who states the ideal, the unattainable, the unfixed. Ménalque describes the thesis of Gide's momentary lyricism when he says that he is never satisfied with having been happy. The new moment for him must come from oblivion of the past, from renouncement of the past. Throughout *L'Immoraliste* the hero is seeking the discovery of a new moment (in all its forced and necessary purity) before it gives way to the next moment.

This search for the present moment and its accompanying fullness is related in the thought of Gide to the other kind of present which is attached to the past. That present which ties a man to the rigors of the past is dictated by the family. The power of the family, for Gide, leads to an evil conscience and self-betrayal. To be true to himself, the hero must be different from his family. Loyalties both to the family and marriage must be denied. Gide bases his authority for such a belief on the words of Christ Himself: "Let the dead bury the dead"; "who is my mother, who are my brothers?" The family fixes and defines happiness, its happiness. But Gide says that we never seek happiness; we seek the freedom for what is newest in ourselves. Michel's action supports this theory. He renounces the pattern of life which his father had devised for him and seeks to renounce the feeling of gratitude he has for his wife Marcelline.

In Joyce's *Portrait of the Artist as Young Man*, Stephen's thoughts of being sundered from his father precede his first sexual experience, his "loveless lust," as he calls it. It is unreal, but it will separate him from his family. His desire to sin comes from his own soul. If he succeeds in having this experience, he will be solely responsible for his own destruction. This Catholic conception of sin is absent from the work of Gide. Michel wants to commit acts contrary to convention in order to discover himself, and Stephen sins in order to destroy himself. Both seek liberty. Both challenge life with heroic gestures.

Hamlet, as Catholically conscious as Stephen, does not seek to destroy himself by sin, but rather to correct the wrongs of sin with the heroism of moral conviction. He has been cut off from his family in two ways: first, by the death of his father, and secondly, by what he considers the sin of his mother. The characterization of Hamlet as hero is essentially different from that of Michel and Stephen, because he doesn't have to strive alone to be himself. Circumstances force him into solitude. No need to revolt against his family, because his family has departed from him. The sole struggle of the contemporary hero seems to be the struggle to wrest himself from duties, loves, obligations, from all that is not himself, in order to discover what he himself is. The classical hero appears at the outset stripped of all that entangles the conscience of the modern hero. Both seek to know, at grave risks, the experience of their souls: Hamlet, in an effort to furnish his life with moral honesty; Michel and Stephen, in an effort to disburden themselves of whatever becomes dissimilar to their growing and changing natures.

In the early stages of Michel's convalescence at Biskra, he watches the Arab boy Moktir steal a pair of scissors and pretends that he has seen nothing. Later, Ménalque talks with Moktir and discovers that the boy knew Michel had seen him steal. The theft itself was the gratification of liberty. The boy was doubly clever in stealing the scissors and in hiding the fact that he knew he had been caught. This episode of the scissors is a symbol of the precarious sensualism if Michel. (Here we are reminded of the infantalism of Proust, which was perhaps the secret of his genius and which permitted him to rebuild the multiple universe of a child.) Because the conscience of a child does not remember for long the weight of any act, it becomes for Gide the symbol of liberty, the instrument for liberty—and for his immoralist hero it is the symbol of mystery and ardor. Choice is necessary, says Ménalque. But the difficult task is to know what one wants. "Il faut choisir. L'impor-

tant, c'est de savoir ce que l'on veut." The child always
knows what he wants at each moment of his consciousness,
even if there is no reason for it and even if the object of his
desires changes from one moment to the next. Michel longs
for no other conscience than that of a child. Michel, like all
the heroes of Gide, remains bathed in the reflection of those
who have attained the ideal.

His particular concupiscence is a longing for the beauty,
the suppleness, and the freedom which disappeared forever
when he ceased being a youth. All that fills his life as a
man—his marriage, his estate in Normandy, his teaching,
his house at Passy—turns against him and crushes him in
much the same way that fate opposed the ancient hero. His
longing for beauty and freedom is really concupiscence of
the flesh which he doesn't acknowledge but which he prepares unwittingly. The immoralist régime is never lived
and the new love is never consummated. The book prepares
tragedy as the modern world seems to be preparing it.

The tragedy of bourgeois convention is for Gide what
the tragedy of conscience is for Joyce's hero Stephen. The
moral force of sin is on Stephen. As a boy he loved God
and as a man he never recovers from "his loveless awe of
God." Stephen knows, as every Catholic does, that one sin
leads to all sins through the power of the imagination
which, once corrupted, spreads contagion. His mind, once
pure, becomes an orgy after the experience of one sin.
Michel's tragedy is the impossibility of knowing the sensualism which he defines as being his. Stephen, more positive than Michel, commits the one sin which he knows will
liberate him from his innocent past and is henceforth
haunted by the spectres of this one sordid act.

Hamlet is a very distant brother of these two modern

heroes, but a brother, because all three are striving to escape. Hamlet, from shame. Stephen and Michel, from their immediate past which they believe unnatural. What unites them as spiritual brothers is the torture each undergoes. This torture comes from the knowledge of the sins of others. For Michel, it is the carefree life of the senses which he observes in the Arab boys; for Stephen, it is the promiscuity of prostitutes; for Hamlet, it is the new marriage of his mother which he considers adultery. The sin of the flesh is one of the eternal ingredients of tragedy. If no act is consummated (as in the case of Hamlet), there remains always the example of others to torture the hero and the violence thereby perpetrated on his imagination. In such cases, the tragic problem seems to be: Can man rid himself of the slow and secret workings of his conscience? And if man's conscience can be disburdened of the memory of sin or the desire for sin, for what use is the resultant freedom? No hero in tragedy has ever answered this question. Tragedy cannot be established in freedom. It cannot move except within the bounds of conscience. The greatest form which literature can take is the depiction of this realm of tragedy in which the hero's knowledge of good and evil is the lonely protagonist bent upon self-destruction or self-realization.

Lust, then, appears inevitably as one of the ingredients of tragedy, and the hero in contemporary literature believes that he must prepare himself for it minutely by heroism (if heroism is a surpassing of oneself). In older tragedy, this ingredient is minor; it is almost a kind of perfume. Hamlet, Antigone, Le Cid abandon passion for passionate duty. Their passion is not insistent; it awaits a calmer period while the heroes strive to conquer a different kind of world: Hamlet, to commit murder; Antigone, to bury her dead; Le Cid, to justify a murder. Ancient tragedy did not attempt to depict death as much as it attempted to depict the justification of death. And, conversely, modern tragedy does not seem so bent upon portraying life as it does upon a justification of life.

(The humanism of the Renaissance has maintained and developed to its logical conclusion throughout the entire modern era its fundamental lesson, which is the lesson of man facing himself and his human destiny. This lesson has taught the modern hero to give no more thought to his supernatural destiny which alone can raise a moral issue to an heroic level.)

The modern hero, that is, the "immoralist," seeks to know whom he can love and rarely approaches the conception of a tragic gesture, because the tragic gesture can be made only when one knows whom one loves. He undergoes the tragedy of passion and rarely attains that tragedy which emerges from the conflict between moral conviction and the world.

The Gidian hero believes that every joy awaits him. But it awaits him *alone*. He must give up everything else in order to experience any one joy. Joy is a kind of jealous prostitute who insists upon a bargain. The minute she gives eradicates all other minutes. No other modern literary work illustrates better than Gide's the mediaeval lesson that the practice of evil changes completely a man's loyalty and transforms completely his human nature. Michel contemplates one form after another of joy. He seems to have recovered his health in order to contemplate a daily joy. As he grows in health and fluctuating desires, his wife Marcelline declines in health. But how colorless in the literary

work is this picture of her fidelity! Gide's art forces us to
heed very little the character who, in another age, would
have been the tragic character. Marcelline's suffering is
never an audible theme in *L'Immoraliste*. The work grows
around the disquietude of Michel who is unable to assume
the responsibility for any deep suffering. The titular hero
seems to become important by his very desertion of heroism.

This transposition of tragedy—or transposition of the
tragic sense from the hero to a secondary character—seems
to be, in one way, a key to Gide's work and the literary
work of most contemporary artists. The modern hero
lives in a kind of reflection of tragedy, but separated from
its responsibility and pathos. The illness of Marcelline, in
L'Immoraliste, from which she is unable to recover and
which ends with her death in the second half of the novel,
is in all respects comparable to the fate of the classical
hero. Marcelline, even if she isn't the protagonist, rises to
the stature of tragedy and assumes unto herself all the
guilt of Michel who, although he is the hero, escapes the
weight of any tragic sense of life.

Michel, at one point in the story, becomes a poacher
on his own estate and learns something of the voluptuousness of watching in the dark for prey which it isn't lawful
to seize. He thus forces himself to become another character in order to forget that he himself really owns the ani-
mals which he is trying to kill or trap. This experience in
falsehood, which the immoralist undertakes in order to be
truthful to his desires, corresponds to the theft of the scissors in the first part of the book. Bared of all its superficial connotations, the episode seems to depict Michel's
desire to possess a love which will exact no loyalty. Gide,

the clear thinker, the sage, the sensitive artist, adjusts the words of Holy Scripture to his conscience as his heroes adjust the acts of their lives to the daily newnesses of their desires. The hero doesn't feel the opposition of fate as much as he feels the crumbling of fate, when he relegates to his wife, to his family, to the past, to heredity, all the constraining bonds of his conscience.

Rather than strengthening himself in order to meet his fate and elaborate his soul during the encounter, the Gidian hero prepares himself for the suppleness necessary to meet a new fate each day. His fate is unknown, unspecified, improvised. This is the major reason why the surrealists have always admired Gide. The classical hero, whether it be Oedipus or Hamlet, rises toward light and order; his tragedy is the collapse of these goals. But the Gidian hero intoxicates himself with night and anarchy. His soul is made into a scapegoat—the bearer of philosophies he had once heeded in another age—while his body remains in the immediate literary work, alone and vulnerable.[8]

IV

When we alluded first to the character of Gide, we tried to describe, above all, his sincerity, which of course is a form of heroism. Then, in the creation of one of his heroes we have just seen a vain form of heroism, the portrait of a man standing in the shadow of heroism because of the particular learning and science of his age and because of the moral nimbleness of his creator. Now, we should like to point out a further kind of heroism, that of Gide as an artist. The writer's heroism is an authentic one and peculiar to our age. In the group of modern novelists who have been most conscious of their art and most scrupulous in the defining of their vocation: James, Proust, Joyce—André Gide occupies an outstanding place. All his life he has been concerned with what it means to be an artist and with how to transform life into art. Most of his writing seems to prove that he welcomed any experience which could be synthesized into words, as though literature were the raison d'être for experience.[4]

It is not exaggerated to say that Gide forced himself to write through a belief in the hygiene of writing. The moral and amoral exercises of his character are quite similar to his habits as a writer. At those moments when he felt himself least able to write, when his mind seemed completely empty of ideas, he would force himself to write a few lines in his journal about anything at all. Like Flaubert he knew the exhausting struggle over the writing of a page of prose, and like Flaubert he could easily convince himself that when he was composing, he was working in the absolute. The true meaning of a work of art for Gide is in its form. This is why different books could come from his mind and why his resemblance is impossible to catch. As soon as the writing of a book was completed, he was already more different from that book than from any other. His writer's hygiene forced him to acknowledge to himself each morning that the most important book still remained for him to write and that it was high time for him to begin it.

This general courage of Gide in the art of writing is accompanied by a severe stylistic discipline and purification. If we do not forget his original romantic nature, we shall realize the heroism he has manifested in the evolution of his language which has been progressively simplified and chastened. From the tearfulness of *André Walter*, which he wrote at twenty, to the perfected soberness of the pages written fifty years later, Gide has made a pilgrimage toward the belief that any ornament in a work hides some defect. Gide has said that when he wrote *André Walter* he hadn't yet learned how to write in French, and at sixty he said that it was time for him to learn all over again how to write in French. He believes that all the best contemporary writers are precious. I am convinced that he has always considered Marcel Proust to be the master of dissimulation. Heroically, Gide first defined what his salvation as a writer would consist of—and then he labored persistently to save himself. This salvation seems to reside in the attainment to a poverty of words, to a diminished language. Gide is fearful of the power which words have to generate a sentiment of their own, which will not be the sentiment of the author.

V

This study began with mention of the puritanism of Gide's childhood and this theme will serve us, in a sense, for our conclusion in which we should like to describe still another form of heroism: the heroism of Gide as a Frenchman. To emerge a Frenchman after beginning life as a Puritan is a great victory. What are the outstanding ways in which Gide has emulated the French ideal and contributed to the resilience of the French tradition?

First, of course, Gide's perpetual study of form and style in writing is a French trait. A sense of clarity and proportion, an ability to choose a length suitable to the development of each of his themes and an awareness of the detail to omit as well as the detail to elaborate, have helped him to join in perfect union, idea and form. Two French writers whose names appear often in his journal and whom he has always read with special joy and profit are two of the greatest masters of French style: Bossuet and Racine. Whereas Bossuet ravished him in almost a sensuous way with his fullness and harmony and force, Racine gave him the emotion of perfection, a joy purer than he could derive from any other writer. Shakespeare appeared more human, but Racine represented the triumph of a convention, "le triomphe d'une convenance"—and any art form is after all a convention.

Gide is peculiarly French in his appreciation of foreign writers and in the kind of influence they have had upon him. Three writers above all have been associated with the work of Gide: Dostoievsky, Nietzsche, and Freud. It is quite safe to say that Gide's thought would be the same if he had never known them. In them he found authorization rather than enlightenment. All three were always to some degree in his nature, and when he did come to know their texts directly, he was able to assimilate their teaching and adapt it to his own in that remarkably subtle and inoffensive way which has permitted the French to turn foreign influences into something French. Gide inherited the French genius of enriching himself with a foreign influence while retaining the totally French quality of his own work. Critics have often pointed out the Nietzschean themes in *L'Immoraliste*, but as a matter of fact, Gide was already writing *L'Immoraliste* when he first came upon the text of Nietzsche.

Then, secondly, Gide's preoccupation with psychological and moral problems is a French preoccupation. On the whole, from the Middle Ages to the twentieth century, from *La Chanson de Roland* to the most recent novels of

Mauriac and Malraux, French literature has been more concerned with men than with nature and more concerned with man than with men. Gide, like his two predecessors whom he has admired and read all his life, Montaigne and Pascal, has consecrated his thought to the multiple problems of man as an individual in society, to the understanding of man's freedom and man's servitude, to the eternal debate between man's soul and man's body. The stories and novels of Gide, like the essays of Montaigne and the *Pensées* of Pascal, are crossroads or meeting-places of problems. Whether it is in the words of Christ or in the writings of Marx, Gide has relentlessly sought the key to the meaning of man's dignity.

Then, in the third place, Gide as a writer in his relations with the world, has been fearless. Always, in France, the great writer of each period—and, it almost seems, in order to be great—has had to place himself firmly within his civilization to reveal the civilization to itself and point out for it its true direction. This often has entailed opposition and even bitter suffering. The prison of Villon, the solitude and estrangement of Molière, the exile of Victor Hugo, the voyages of Rimbaud can all be explained in various ways, but they are also symbols of the artist's fate. Gide has never been afraid of his adversaries. In fact, he is more afraid of those who have sought to defend him because he has not tried to reveal his thought to others but to reveal their thought to themselves. If much of the poetry and philosophy of today is dead because it is separated from life, Gide's thought grows in intensity for us because it has always participated in life. The artist must oppose his time by being of it more deeply than other men. He must be the initiator.

During this present period of silence and humiliation, France is contemplating the heroism of her past and is beginning to realize that she is not even now bereft of every form of heroism. As late as 1931 Gide wrote that what contemporary literature lacks the most, is heroism. But this awareness may well be the first step toward a new age, and when that age comes about, through a combination of a Gidian heroism and a more traditional one, it will have heeded the lesson of the writer of our age about whom we can truthfully say: "Behold a man in whom there is no guile."

FRANÇOIS MAURIAC:
The Catholic Tradition

I

FRANÇOIS MAURIAC belongs to the generation of French
writers born between two other generations: the first, including Claudel, Gide, Proust, and Valéry, all of whom
were born about 1870; and the last generation, born with
the century, including such writers as Malraux, Giono,
Saint-Exupéry. Of those mentioned in the oldest living
generation, only Proust is dead, and all four unquestionably
have their place in the highest rank of French letters. (In
richness and brilliance only one other group is comparable,
that born about 1622, which includes La Fontaine, Molière,
and Pascal.) Mauriac's own generation, born about 1885,
has given many celebrated names: Roger Martin du Gard,
Giraudoux, Duhamel, Jules Romains—but already the test
of years seems to be assigning him the first place of importance.

His work is very large: three volumes of verse, almost
twenty novels, almost twenty volumes of literary criticism,
a play, and three volumes of his journal. It is difficult to
realize the extent of Mauriac's published work because his
style is sober and restrained. It seems to be a work written
after meditation and thought, of a kind which would pre-
clude abundant and sustained expression. The number of
titles is perhaps misleading. Almost all of his books are

47

brief; most of his novels are the usual length of the long novella; his literary studies and essays are of minimum length. He has been publishing with marked regularity and frequency since 1909 and has evidently passed through no salient period of dryness or infecundity. His work, maintaining its permanent feature of sobriety, has added to itself with regularized persistence for over thirty years, and, as in the classical tradition, this work subsumes the man and the man's life. One thinks of Mauriac's work and not of Mauriac. He has revealed himself to his public, not through spectacular demonstration, or scandal, or lectures, or social functions, but through the characters of his stories and the mental exercises of his criticism. We don't think of Mauriac, but rather of Mauriac's sensitivity and Mauriac's understanding of human nature. The man has been concealed by the novelist; the personality has been concealed by the intellect and the intellect's honest operations. This is more than modesty; it is a trait of nobility and intactness which James Joyce had also during his lifetime.

Mauriac is essentially the novelist, the psychological novelist who discovers his realism in the secret motivations and desires of his characters. His critical writings almost all deal with the craft of the novelist and the mysterious process of creating characters out of one's memory and sensitivity. His novels are his direct creation and his principle concern; his criticism is a modern form of "confession" in which he painfully and humbly analyses his art in terms of his conscience and his faith. His novels are the acts of his life; his criticism is their commentary, their reasoned and inspired justification. Frequently he has acknowledged that his characters are masks of himself and that the art of writing is in reality the art of revealing oneself.

Since Rousseau, literary masks have worn thin until in many cases they fail to conceal the literal features, the flesh and blood features of the hero behind them. Hamlet and Cleopatra were masks and stylized projections of Shakespeare, as were Phèdre and Antiochus for Racine. But since the romantic spell in literature, it has become increasingly difficult for the artist to project himself beyond himself. His masks are himself as a child, as an adolescent, as a young man. A world is created in a modern novel, but it is usually familiar and autobiographical. The novel is therefore the expansion, the personalization, and in a certain sense perhaps, the degeneration of tragedy.

"Ecrire, c'est se livrer" Mauriac could therefore write at the beginning of his essay on *Dieu et Mammon*, and call up to mind the verse of Claudel in which the writer is grouped with the assassin and the whore. They all have their price and give themselves to their paying clients. One has the conviction that Mauriac is always at the very center of his novels, although it is impossible to point him out literally anywhere in them. There is an alliance between him and his characters. They are of his own flesh, yet they are also different from him. This close unity (in a spiritual order) and this separateness (in a literary order) of Mauriac and his characters cause his novels, more than any other contemporary novels, to resemble tragedies. They have the unbreathable atmosphere of tragedies and they are composed with a tragic lyricism which comes from the close bond existing between the creator and his creatures, from Mauriac's marriage with his created destinies. No space stretches out between Mauriac and his pages; no distance between Mauriac and his characters permits them to have uncontrolled existences.

II

The one note of a personal character that has been attached to Mauriac is his Catholicism. He is known as a
"Catholic" novelist, although in that particular category
he occupies a special rank which has mystified his critics
and readers. His writing is not pietistic, it is psychological.
His writing is shorn of didacticism, of proselytism, of vapid
wonderment and sobs and sighs in the presence of Catholic
doctrine and ritual. His faith is deep and greater than himself; the truth upon which his faith relies is deeper and
more abundant than his faith. The weaknesses and suffering
of man are the subjects of his novels (as they are, in some
way or other, of all art), and the theme of sainthood, absent from his books, were it sounded, would cause the
pages to close and the artist to stop his search.

Catholicism is a philosophy and a way of life which has
lived in Mauriac and with which Mauriac has lived without
interruption. He was born into it, without his having chosen
it. It was imposed upon him at the beginning of his life and
he has never separated himself from it. Mauriac began
with the Catholic faith and didn't have to discover it. He
has written about watching, one day in the chapel of a
Benedictine convent on the rue Monsieur in Paris, two
recent converts, Ernest Psichari and Jacques Maritain, two
men for whom Catholicism had been a choice—and mar-
veling at the experience which they had undergone and
which would never be known to him. It is very important
to remember that Mauriac's Catholicism is not that of a
convert, acquired after struggle and renouncement and
decision, which must be explained and made radiant to the
world he has left.

Mauriac, therefore, is not the apostle for Catholicism, and his writings bear no trace of didactic or doctrinal usefulness. He is an artist. And his books, as they have appeared one after the other, testify to the effortlessness and disinterestedness of true art: the appearance of effortlessness which is the final stamp and achievement of labor; the stark value of disinterestedness which is unmeasurable and which assures life to a work of art in making it independent of the artist and of the artist's philosophy.

The world of Mauriac's novels is the ancient and contemporary site of man's struggle between good and evil. The Catholic nature is not exempt from the combat between God and man's passion, for it is the human nature in which the combat will show its sharpest contours and appear in its most lurid light. The Catholic nature can maintain simultaneously the certainty of its faith and the fear of all of its race which at times in its history did not have faith. The ancient terror of man alone in the presence of his passions lives in the memory and experience of the Catholic. He is not severed from the responsibility and history of the past as other modern men may be. He knows, more implicitly than other men will acknowledge, that suffering— the ancient suffering of mankind which is essentially metaphysical in nature—has given man his features and the traits of his mind and the heroism he may discover at rare intervals in his heart. Mauriac is not interested in the physical climate of his novels, nor in their human climate; he is solely interested in the complicity between the two climates, in the pattern which they form when engaged together, in the significant struggle which is generated from their commingling.

The ancient world of the heart, then, is Mauriac's world.

Within it we can observe the lesser provincial world of Bordeaux and the Landes. The pine trees, the birds that are hunted, the closed lonely houses, the trains coming from Paris or returning to Paris which cut through the night and shake the shutters and window panes are the elements of the physical climate in Mauriac's novels and they exist only in relation to the characters who own the pine trees, hunt the birds, smell the odors of the closed up houses, and listen to the trains screeching in the night.

The solitude of the heart's world is Mauriac's major theme. His understanding of tragedy is that of Racine's Phèdre and Hermione and Corneille's Infante, the tragedy of a man loving the one being in the world who is unable to love him. It is the total tragedy of love, as stark as the desolate Landes and the setting for *Bérénice*. Jean Péloueyre, the hero of *Le Baiser aux Lépreux*, is typical of Mauriac's heroes. Throughout the story, the destruction of Péloueyre's heart is gradually accomplished as the abyss grows between him and his wife. His physical appearance is pitiful and ugly. He knows that he causes in his wife feelings of disgust and pity, and heroically he removes himself from her side. In a certain sense, Jean Péloueyre is the new type of tragic hero, comparable to Pinocchio, to Charlie Chaplin, and to the creations of Walt Disney. He is the timid ordinary man who appears great by the *grotesqueness* of his suffering. He is the hero who is forced, because of his deformity or plainness, to develop the sense of the poacher or the sense of the animal tracking another animal. He can only hope to spy on the one he loves and look out at her from the darkness of the night and the darkness of his heart. Jean Péloueyre has been called by the critic Ramon Fernandez the "scapegoat" in Mauriac's work. And we might call him the scapegoat of the modern tragic heroes: Pinocchio, Charlie Chaplin, the reluctant dragon, Leopold Bloom, Marcel in *Albertine Disparue*, Edouard in *Les Faux-Monnayeurs*, Aschenbach in *Death in Venice*. In all these heroes, the tragic defect, which Aristotle poses as requirement for the tragic hero, has become so magnified that it is the rule and the nature. They do not have to perform any specific act in order to be heroic; to live and to continue living is their form of heroism. There is no crisis in their lives as there is for Oedipus and Othello and Polyeucte; their daily existence stretches out as an uninterrupted tedium of suffering.

Tragedy has been forced to change its form into that of the novel because the crisis of the hero's life, which is the symbol and concentration of his greatness, has ceased to be true in the modern world where the danger into which he is thrown exists every hour. The tragic play deals with the danger for the hero of losing at one moment his greatness. The tragic novel deals with the inevitability and permanence of the hero's danger. Danger is not, therefore, for the modern hero, a threat of existence but a mode of existence. A great tragedy (like a justified war) is destined to achieve its completion in a tone and atmosphere of moral serenity. Our great modern novels are unable to achieve this because their tragic state is unresolved. The only serenity which they attain is what might be called a poetic serenity.

Action for Jean Péloueyre in Mauriac's novel is an avoidance of the action which in the ordinary sense would be termed "heroic." Other modern literary heroes and Mauriac's characters refute the eighteenth century doctrine of progress. They represent the immobility and the invaria-

of good or of evil; and the one as perilous as the other.
For Mauriac, man exists solely in the peril of evil. He
knows that God is not a character for the novelist. The men
and women whom the novelist creates out of his own flesh
and blood and out of the turmoil of his heart are those who
resist God. The birth of sainthood, even the temptation
to sainthood, would cause art to end for such a novelist as
Mauriac. As a Christian, he understands the final silence of
Pascal, of Racine, and even of Rimbaud. As a novelist he
knows that any interpretation of that silence would be futile, and in a sense, unlawful.

The silence of these men is not the emptiness Mauriac
feels in the world which Proust created. "Dans l'humanité
proustienne, ce qui me frappe, c'est ce creux, ce vide, enfin
l'absence de Dieu." The silence of Racine and perhaps that
of Rimbaud is the shift from one world to another. The
characters of Racine living according to their natures and
Arthur Rimbaud living according to his nature, underwent
a mysterious interruption, broke off their literary existences, and entered a period of silence. A novelist like
Mauriac could interpret this as a shift from living according
to man's nature to living according to the opposite principle: grace. But the characters of Mauriac do not consent
to silence and to the fact that God can exact of a human
being nothing less than everything. Racine and Rimbaud
cease being writers when they resign themselves to solitude. Pascal and Proust never resigned themselves to
solitude, but the words which fill the world of Pascal
describe the fall of man and the source of his disorder,
whereas the words which fill the world of Proust describe
the disorder of man and retain no reminiscence of its source.

Mauriac the novelist seems literally to solicit the source

of what a Freudian psychologist would call man's disorder and what a Christian theologian would call man's sin. The chaos of man's life is given in Mauriac's writing an order and a focus; but this inner life is not controlled by him, it is described by him. Pascal was able to contemplate both the source of man's disorder and the great purity of man's first creation, but Mauriac, who is a novelist, has to limit himself to the sole dignity of sin, that is, the dignity of men who do not know that they desire, who do not love what they think they love. This is the testimonial of the hero in one of Mauriac's most finished novels, *Le Noeud de Vipères*: "Nous ne savons pas ce que nous désirons, nous n'aimons pas ce que nous croyons aimer." The heart that is known is described by the very title of the book, the "vipers' nest." Mauriac and Pascal join one another in their belief that man is man only in order to dream of becoming a saint. Even if Mauriac's characters have lost their sense of familiarity with the things of heaven, they are familiar with their own human natures and hence have that troubled longing for heaven through the very abandonment which their hearts perceive daily.

Pascal and Mauriac have revealed the deepest and most vital parts of themselves. The *pensées* of the one and the novels of the other represent a kind of interminable dialogue during which nothing that counts is hidden. It is the dialogue of disorders which are both perilous and sublime. Pascal's soul is that of ancient Jacob struggling with the angel, but his is a more knowing soul than Jacob's. Pascal is the poet of ideas and Mauriac is the poet of characters. The bareness of the ideas and the solitude of the characters cause them to appear as the products of a Jansenist mind, but if Pascal and Mauriac have a Jansenist temperament, they never submit to a pure Jansenist belief. Pascal retains his liberty in ideas as well as his belief in human liberty, and Mauriac maintains the liberty of his characters even if they have repudiated what he as a Christian would define as the true source of their liberty.

Maritain has accused Mauriac of Manicheism and Gide has accused Mauriac of a desire to love God without losing sight of Mammon. Mauriac's answer to such accusations, which he accepts in part and in a certain sense, is that as a novelist he has a kind of liberty which is analogous to the liberty of a Christian. It is not the power of sin which he exalts in his writings but rather the dignity which an awareness of sin confers upon a human being. As Bach represents the triumph of the mind over numbers, so does Mauriac represent the triumph of the mind over sin. For numbers, in the world of Bach, become sound; and sin, in the world of Mauriac, becomes action and the explanation of human liberty.

Flaubert's blasphemy against life is never uttered by Mauriac. Nor is Alceste's blasphemy against the world, in Molière's *Le Misanthrope,* ever uttered by Mauriac. Alceste's desert to which he is going, is the symbol of the classical hero's pride. He is the type of hero who leaves the world because of its imperfections, in order to take refuge in a desert, whereas Jean Péloueyre and the other characters of Mauriac, are they themselves the desert.

IV

Mauriac and Gide are together, and apart from other contemporary writers, in the eminent gift of their natures which is perhaps best designated by the word "sympathie." They appear as one in their comprehension and

in their awareness of man's deepest problems. They diverge
in their belief about man's freedom of self-development:
Gide represents the supple mind of a general catholicity in
his admonitions to develop the entire man and the entire
personality at the expense of any fixed system; Mauriac
represents the concentrated mind of historical Catholicism
in his prayers to develop a single part of man which will
subsume his personality within the limits (which are bound-
less, in a metaphysical sense) of a fixed doctrine.

Each day for Gide is the recommencing of his belief and
his experience, or rather of a new belief which will emerge
from a new experience. "Il ne se passe guère de jour que
je ne remette tout en question." (*Journal*, p. 744.) His
honesty is a lonely form of sincerity; his restlessness is the
solitude of his intelligence. He is alone always in his awak-
ening to each day and he remains vulnerable to the newness of each day. This newness of each day Gide would
never define, as Mauriac would, in terms of the renewed
daily insistence of God's love. In Mauriac's consciousness
everything has been crystalized about the notions of purity,
sin, and state of grace. Mauriac, as a Catholic, believes that
both man's purity and his sin are due to his freedom of
choice and result from his freedom of will. Man's state
of grace comes from God gratuitously but does not contradict or remove his human freedom. These terms of purity,
sin, and state of grace have been merged in Gide's understanding of human freedom which he designates by the
term "disponibility." To be free, according to Gide, is to
be free to receive all experiences and thoughts not as values in themselves, but as values in the development of
human life. To be free, according to Mauriac, is to be free
to distinguish between good and evil and to realize that

the development of human life takes place only through good.

In a very real sense, then, Gide has reason to call Mauriac the tormented one and the restless one ("l'inquiet et le tourmenté"). God's collaboration which Gide believes to exist in every work of art ("cette part d'inconscient, que je voudrais appeler la part de Dieu—Un livre est toujours une collaboration." *Paludes*, p. 9), has perhaps a kind of analogy with the necessary collaboration which exists between the reader and the author. Mauriac feels more acutely than Gide his writer's responsibility, but both know that a great book is a violent act and that it is impossible to move a reader without in some way causing him grief.

Gide and Mauriac, both as revolutionary as artists can be, are lucidly representative of the contemporary moment in the history of man, whose events may lead us sorrowfully to acknowledge that there has been little moral progress since the Middle Ages. They both believe—Mauriac more profoundly than Gide, because Mauriac's individualism is nearer that of the mediaeval artisan—that artists do not produce the work they would like to, but rather the work they deserve to. ("On n'écrit pas le livre qu'on veut mais on écrit, hélas! le livre qu'on mérite." *Dieu et Mammon*, p. 165.)

The "récits" and the journal of Gide, the novels and the criticism of Mauriac, are two evenly divided works, two forms of the modern artist's *summa*. Gide has been solicited all his life by his Catholic friends to bend to the morality of the Church. And Mauriac has been suspected all his life by his Catholic friends of having exalted the sins of man and of having tricked, in some mysterious way, Christian morality. Both are endowed with a French heart: Gide, with a heart which is reminiscent of Montaigne; and Mauriac, with a heart reminiscent of Pascal. Yet it is the same heart in its activity, which scrutinizes man, his soul, his destiny, his secret. Both find, in this exploration of man, what they wish to find there: Gide, the need for a liberation in order to serve God; Mauriac, the need for a capitulation in order to serve God.

JULES ROMAINS:
The Novel of Good Will and the World of Evil

I

THE PUBLICATION OF *Les Hommes de Bonne Volonté* has been going on for a decade. In 1932 the first volume appeared in Paris; in 1941 the nineteenth and twentieth volumes were published in New York. This long work, which prophesies and describes the major world events between 1908 and 1922, has itself been affected by the present war, and the publication of the French edition continues here in the United States. The "roman-fleuve" is not a new genre in French literature, but it is quite safe to say that the Romains work is destined to surpass all other examples in magnitude. Already there are twenty-one volumes; 6,172 pages; almost 800 characters; a span of fourteen years in the story; elaborate descriptions of Paris, London, Rome, Nice, Odessa; portraits of Jaurès, Briand, Merry del Val; Poincaré, Lenin, Kaiser Wilhelm II, Joffre, Pétain; the juxtaposition of various worlds: the army, the Church, the political scene, the medical world, the French Academy; all the familiar themes of the novel: love, crime, pathos, worldliness, friendship, the greatness of obscure and humble characters, the selfishness and pride of the mighty. The literary enterprise is gigantic, and it is impossible to tell how many more volumes are to be published *

* M. Romains stated in the summer of 1941 that he plans to have 27 volumes in his work.

or whether M. Romains intends to catch up with history. Critical judgments of this work have not been slow in appearing, both favorable and adverse. The size already attained in the published part justifies perhaps a pause in the reading and an attempt to place the novel in the career of Romains and to consider the particular form of art it represents.

II

Without any doubt, *Les Hommes de Bonne Volonté* is to be Romains' central work. He has said so himself in his preface to the first volume. But his first important book, published in 1908—the year he chose to open the story of his novel—was poetry; in fact, he has published five or more volumes of poetry, and his most recent, *L'Homme Blanc*, of 1937, interrupted the publication of his novel. It is in the lyricism of this early poetry, *La Vie Unanime*, that Romains states the initial impulse of his sensitivity which has grown into a complicated verbalism in his mature writing. "Unanimism" is his own word, his own formula, the theme of his early poetry and the key to his recent prose. The unanimist feels the poetry of the whole: of the whole street, of the whole city, of all humanity. He is not an individual looking at the world and being moved by it; rather, he is a part of the whole and feels the movement of the whole because he is so closely merged with it. He feels the reality of the street and the city and the group because his personal feelings have been absorbed in them. If he remains one, he will be unlimited —like the sponge which never bursts through soaking up an infinity of water. His intimate thoughts and his heart are worthy to be scorned when he contrasts his own dream with the profounder dream of the city. The height of his lyricism is reached when he seizes the happiness of non-being: "Je connais le bonheur de n'être presque pas"; and his soul becomes the street in its various postures of medita-tion: "Mon âme c'est la rue au soir qui se recueille."

Romains was not a student of sociology during the years when he was composing *La Vie Unanime*, between 1904 and 1907. His poetry is not the versified lesson of his teacher Durkheim at Normale because he had written it before reading Durkheim or hearing his voice. Although he graciously sent a copy of his verse to Gustave Le Bon, he had taken care not to read a line of the sociologist. There were two surer masters who inspired the lyrical movement of the young Romains and whose influence is perceptible throughout *Les Hommes de Bonne Volonté*. These masters were Victor Hugo and Paris. They might be coalesced into one: the Paris of Victor Hugo.

The French temperament is periodically assailed by one form or another of preciosity. The most constant is per-haps the lyric expression the French give to the beauty of the city, to the beauty of the parts, of the things of the city: the light of its sky, the form of its trees, the architec-ture of its buildings, the grace of its evenings. The poetic eye sees this so intensely that the stature of man in the city is diminished. This is not true of the greatest artists. Villon and Baudelaire do not sacrifice the drama of man to his habitation. But Victor Hugo and his disciple Jules Romains have made their creatures indistinct one from another in their meditation before the collective force of the city and the collective beauty of its murmur and its color. Their creatures are subdued and live mechanically as under the direction and spell of a very mysterious but omnipotent power. In both Hugo and Romains, the theme may shift from that of the city to that of humanity, but the total effect is the same. The vastness of the power admits an unlimited flow of expression. The poem (or the novel) grows and grows, almost rapidly, without ever striking against an obstacle, without ever seeing a living person. The culminating phrase of Romains' most recent poetry is "Ŏ République Universelle." Victor Hugo had dreamed of the same hope for humanity.

Romains may incline his reader to believe that man is not real, but what he sees, is. Each one of us is dead, he will tell us, and the unanimist life is our sepulchre. During the long course of the novel, Romains has not been unfaithful, in any philosophical sense, to his earliest writing. *Les Hommes de Bonne Volonté* is the application, elaborate, complicated, symmetrical, of the lyric Hugoesque message in *La Vie Unanime*. The poet has made himself into a novelist without relinquishing any of his particular poetic vision of the world.

III

The imposing number of characters who have already appeared in *Les Hommes de Bonne Volonté*—some to take leading parts, some to die, many to have brief introductions and destined perhaps never to return—has made of the novel a vast repertory of men and women and children and even a dog, drawn from every class, who meet or live separately. Each volume introduces new characters many of whom seem to be isolated from those we already know, and new intrigues or enterprises which also seem to bear no relation to the intrigues we are already following. But the scheme of the entire work is intricate and extensive.

Every detail has doubtless been consciously planned, and its reason and relation to the rest will become apparent only with the unfolding of the story. In the treatment of so numerous a world it is quite remarkable that a reader is able to remember most of the characters. They are described with a touch that is sure and clear; they are usually given names that are creations in themselves, e.g. Wazemmes, Havercamp, Champcenais, Saint-Papoul, Maillecottin; we first see them in the performance of some act which henceforth will be associated with them; they will serve not only as instruments in the accomplishment of some act: such as crime, seduction, or political espionage, but they will serve too as a specific tonality or picturesque motif which is often the basis of whole passages and essays. Gradually, M. Romains seems to be building up a community where every type will be represented, where every human desire, vice and ambition will have its part, where every profession will be analyzed even in its most tedious details. A bookbinder, a spinster, a countess, a writer, a prime minister, a general, a student, a priest, a physician, a teacher, a business man, a cardinal, a workman, a pimp: the list could be extended indefinitely and the characters who make it up would not be confused as concerns their physical characteristics, their vocation, and their most insistent desires. The triumph of clarity in the novel of Jules Romains has been achieved.

What effect does the unanimist treatment of characters have on the psychological development of a work of art, such as a novel? The simple answer to such a question seems to be that the psychological development of Romains' characters is superficial. In trying to discover what philosophy of man Romains incorporates in his work, we are forced to admit that unanimism tends to destroy the possibility of any philosophy because it tends to destroy the individual. The skill with which Romains is able to evoke the unit or the group: the banlieue-nord of Paris, the ecclesiastical world of a provincial bishop, the Ecole Normale on the rue d'Ulm—is not maintained in the psychological motivation or drama of the characters who inhabit these various worlds. They are largely automotons or servants of the unit in which they have a place. The color of the unit is their color, the success of the unit is their success; the action of the unit as a whole is the action which they follow irrevocably.

What remains of an individual when subjected to such treatment is an over-simplified characterization, a picturesque one, usually pathetic and almost always sexually motivated. M. Romains is obsessed with the sex impulse and the sexual adventures of his characters. If some have no real carnal adventures, they have dreams and thoughts of physical possession. Even the dog Macaire, who serves as one of the most humorous motifs in the work, has a dramatic although abortive love escapade. But if sex is the permanent basis for Romains' psychological dissertations, it also is treated as though it were a unit in the unanimistic régime, implacable and commanding. An overwhelming portion of the literary work is consecrated to erotic didacticism. Sex is monotonously the same experience with a countess, a student, a dog, and a minister of foreign relations. The pattern of courtship and amorous capitulation is stated over and over again with no psychological variations. The adulterous scene with the worldly Marie de Champcenais (vol. 5) is described with the same hesitations and thoughts as is the ancillary scene of the young priest

Mionnet (vol. 8) and the very specially prepared scene of assault with the novelist-critic Allory (vol. 11). At times it would appear that the various groups and separate intrigues of the novel will be united and given coherence thanks to the similar sex urge in all seven hundred characters and the resultant irregular sexual relations.

The problem of the hero in *Les Hommes de Bonne Volonté* is mysterious. And yet not mysterious when one considers that the rules of unanimism do not provide for a hero. (Soon critics will be saying that Paris is the hero of this novel, as they have said that the cathedral is the real hero of *Notre Dame de Paris.*) Several of the volumes have given most of their pages to one character: Quinette, the bookbinder, in the second volume; Louis Bastide, the child, in the sixth; Viaur, the doctor, in the twelfth; Jallez, the writer, in the eighteenth. Only in four of the volumes so far does it seem impossible to name the leading character. But from these various leading characters, will one emerge as hero? Perhaps not. The hero may be the humanity of France in our century. Perhaps it will be a double hero; the two students who meet at Normale in 1908: Jallez from Paris and the provincial Jerphanion. In their conversations and letters Romains has done some of his best writing. Perhaps in their dual portraits he has put himself most faithfully on paper. Together they approach the dimensions of a hero, because together they represent a conflict which is the requirement for heroism: Jerphanion, the submissive man who is teacher, husband, father, soldier, the man who has his designated place in the unit; and Jallez, the dreamer, the poet, the pacifist, the one who is faithful to an ideal love and who fears attachment to anything real. However, the psychological acuteness in this double hero is sacrificed to the neatness of the pattern and ideal of the two diverging natures.

IV

If no hero gives a guiding action and order to *Les Hommes de Bonne Volonté,* the mode of composition gives the work a form of artistic unity. At first one may be confused by the number of lives and scenes which are unrelated, but this rapid cinematographic technique, when prolonged, may end by developing a charm in the very diversity of characters, in the unforeseen freedom of movement with which an entire city is encompassed. The roofs of so many buildings are raised and we see into so many lives which continue unperturbed that the first impression we had of reading an unfinished work changes to a habit of curiosity in the unknown and a tedium with a passage too prolonged.

M. Romains does not wish to create habits of concentrating vision on an individual. As in the life of comets, there must be a pathos in the dispersal of human life, in the insignificance and monotony of human life, in the appearance and subsequent vanishing of a face. He has consciously avoided an ample action, one which is aided by fortuitous meetings of characters and by a miraculously elected champion. "Le roman, lui, ne connaît pas de vraies servitudes," he wrote in his preface to *Les Hommes de Bonne Volonté.* He intended at the outset to oppose the habits of laziness in readers who have learned to follow a classical plot with its one line which is never lost sight of.

The unanimist style is felt above all in the endless brief portraits and silhouettes of the novel, in the intimate scenes between two people, in the many scenes of larger groups

where the writing of Romains concentrates upon delinea-
tion and unimportant but familiar action. Here his art is
alert, clear and humorous, or pathetic according to the situation. It is skill in narration, success in a well-turned exercise. The twenty-second chapter in the fourteenth volume,
Le Drapeau Noir, is an extreme example of the unanimist
style. It is a series of rapid evocations of several characters
who have no relation one to another, all pursuing different
aims and thinking different thoughts at the same hour of
the same day in Paris: the dog Macaire, the student Jallez,
the young woman Juliette, the spinster Mlle. Bernadine,
the dying Lommérie, etc. The chapter is successful picture
telling without any obvious purpose and without any visible
progress.

When the unanimist style is abandoned, the vastness of
the literary project becomes apparent and weighty. In
addition to the care and animation with which Jules Romains has described his characters and their settings is a
constant sense of exactitude and detail. He manifests no
superficiality in the painting of his major worlds: political,
ecclesiastical, masonic, real-estate, military. The facts and
figures of reports are integral parts of his narration. Names,
measurements, hours of the day and night, notes of historical researches appear in close company with more ex-
pansive abstract or lyric notations. The unanimist is also the
documented realist. The installation of the health resort
and clinic at La Celle-des-Eaux (vol. 5) and the battle of
Verdun (vol. 16) are examples of meticulous documenta-
tion which, like the staccato unanimist passages, stand out
as set pieces without demonstrating any particular reason
for their length and precision. The unanimist description
of characters which, above all, places them in their particu-

lar worlds with a particular set of reflexes and the statisti-
cal, full reports on the various worlds both induce, at fre-
quent intervals, Romains the "thinker" to philosophize and
soliloquize. Like appendages on scenes of action or scenes
of description, these essays on love, friendship, poetry, politics, religion, patriotism, sex, street noises—abound and
ɔwarm and reduce the tempo of the work even more than
ιt is already reduced by its multitudinous plots.

The effect of words and sentences accumulating and
propagating themselves is perhaps the major effect of this
long work. The motifs are all of some interest and the
language used is always accessible to a large public, but the
pure verbal pressure which comes from the persistence and
steadiness and flow of words outweighs characters, scenes,
debates, and perceptions. The innumerable small touches
are forgotten in the general movement and sweep which
are "livresques," that is, which seem to be created by the
power of words and the intoxication of sound. The mode
of composition in *Les Hommes de Bonne Volonté* represents a kind of debauchery in rhetoric. It is not the pains-
taking, poignant exploration of Proust. Nor is it the abundant but unified vision of Zola. It is an application of an
innate skill with words on subjects too diversified, too
loosely chosen, too half-heartedly felt.

V

Unanimism is an invention of French origin, and the
"roman-fleuve" or long novel has many distinguished
examples in the history of the French novel. Before the
word "unanimism" was invented, elements of what it defines had already and quite naturally been incorporated into
literary works. Balzac's *Comédie Humaine*, with its large

blocks or divisions of life in the Restoration, subjects its heroes and heroines to the impersonal power of social forces and conventions. (Rastignac contemplates Paris with the same horror and tenderness which Jallez and Jerphanion have in their hearts.) Zola's *Rougon-Macquart* traces the epic story of a family through the generations of the Second Empire and explains the suffering of his creatures in terms of relentless laws of heredity and social injustice. Proust's *A la recherche du temps perdu* limits itself largely to one social class living through the first two decades of the twentieth century, and analyses their moribund complex sensibilities which appear livid in the years subsequent on the period of their true power. But the parts of the *Comédie Humaine* are separate novels and the unity given them by their title remains an exterior unity. Likewise in the long work of Zola, each division has its particular focus and conclusion. Proust's work, however, is a novel and its internal unity comes from its hero. No one of the elaborate passages in the sixteen volumes detracts from Marcel's search for the time of his past.

The "roman-fleuve" of Jules Romains has humorously been called a "roman-caoutchouc" by a critic in the February 1941 number of *Esprit*. Is there a structural plan or unity visible in the groupings of the various volumes or hidden in the true meaning of the title given to the entire work? Until the publication of the nineteenth, the volumes always appeared in groups of two. At the end of the fourth volume there is a letter from the author to his readers which states that these four volumes form the prologue and announce the "organic multiplicity" of things. M. Romains said also that he has planned a carefully symmetrical construction and has resigned himself in advance to the critics' reproach of no plan and haphazard progress in *Les Hommes de Bonne Volonté*. We are convinced that M. Romains knows what he is going to write, but we are also convinced that after reading twenty volumes of a novel, we too should have some opinion concerning its plan and purpose.

It is possible that the first four volumes are a prologue of "organic multiplicity." In them Wazemmes, the young apprentice, loses his virginity in a very natural way; Quinette commits his crime; Jallez narrates his childhood love for Hélène Sigeau; and Jerphanion wanders through the streets of Paris until he meets a young and attractive milliner. Volumes five to twelve continue many other episodes announced in the first four and introduce antitheses in humanity. We meet the successful business man Havercamp in *Les Superbes,* and the young boy, Louis Bastide, timid and poor, of *Les Humbles;* we meet free-masons in *Recherche d'une Eglise,* and the Catholic priest Mionnet (who seems to have little understanding of his faith) in *Province;* we meet the mediocre writer Allory in *Recours à l'Abîme,* and the industrious physician Viaur in *Les Créateurs.* Volumes thirteen to sixteen prepare and describe the first world war. Volumes seventeen to nineteen bring back Quinette, whose murders are beginning to induce insanity; and Jallez, who composes poetry and makes love in Nice; and Clanricard, who in 1922 wearies of teaching and matrimony and is contemplating a trip to Russia, *Cette grande lueur à l'est.* Volume twenty, *Le Monde est ton Aventure,* which appeared in September, 1941, in the "Editions de la Maison Française" of New York, carries the scene into Russia. In Odessa, Jallez and the English journalist Bartlett observe the traces of famine and the *moeurs* of the Soviet Union; in Moscow, Jerphanion and the French minister Bouitton form their first impressions of the Russian state. The final line of the volume announces the imminent reunion of Jallez and Jerphanion.

Perhaps the order of the volumes and their episodes have little importance in the general plan. Perhaps when we discover who the "men of good will" are, the meaning of the work will be clear. It is doubtless false to pick out from this long repertory of human life the characters who do good (as contrasted with those who do evil) and consider them the men of good will. It would be false to put in the first group Louis Bastide, Abbé Jeanne, and Clanricard; and in the second group: Quinette, Abbé Mionnet, and Laulerque. It would also seem erroneous to consider those who submit themselves to society the characters of good will: teachers, priests, workmen; and to consider in the opposite group those who try to rule: politicians, capitalists, artists. The conclusion is forced upon us: all are men of good will. All humanity has goodness no matter how distorted it has become in some individuals. Society is one; men are one. A great event, such as a war, proves it. The novel of Romains is to reflect a great modern city in which thousands of individual lives are spent with daily occupations, loves and hates, but all of which feel certain kindred impulses and are joined mysteriously in the meaning of great events. Romains has Poincaré say in *Mission à Rome*: "Cette guerre-ci (des Balkans) sort en somme, à un an d'intervalle, de la guerre italo-turque, qui se rattachait elle-même à tout ce qui couve dans ce coin de l'Europe depuis octobre 1908, et au-delà."

In the character Quinette, who is a murderer, there are many traits of kindliness and sobriety. If his insanity becomes more pronounced in future volumes, his evil acts will be forgiven him, and our first supposition that he was close to the Gidian type of hero will be false. Romains' abundant use of antitheses, so dear to his master, Hugo, which we first saw in the juxtaposition of characters and scenes, we now see in the juxtaposition of traits within a single character. There may, however, be some danger to unanimism in this explanation. Despite all efforts on the part of their creator, perhaps the heroes will end by claiming what is theirs in a novel which claims in its title to concern itself with human nature.

We must watch the character Pierre Jallez in his future appearances. There is much of both Louis Farigoule and Jules Romains in him. (For Louis Farigoule was once a student at Normale and then became the writer Jules Romains; and Jules Romains remembers that once he was called Louis and perhaps rolled a hoop through the streets of Paris.) Nothing can be prophesied about this "work in progress," but let us continue to follow Jallez who in his very detachment from the characters around him—even from those he loves, and in his philosophical attitude toward events and ideas and matters of the heart, is perhaps destined to succumb as a hero or conquer as a hero. From the susceptible soul of Pierre Jallez we may see the emergence of a hero, or at least the thoughts of a hero, while around him and under him will continue to agitate the hundreds of episodes which he will bring together in some way, at some time.

VI

All such prophecy is tenuous, and it may be stimulated by an effort to make a novel out of *Les Hommes de Bonne*

Volonté when the work really is a genre which claims some place within the loose limits of the novel but whose general literary effect is closer to the traditional effect of another genre. *Les Hommes de Bonne Volonté* is a work of lyricism. The poet of *La Vie Unanime* has recapitulated his first themes, but the action into which he has forced them is so diffuse that the force and unifying focus which action in a novel should have are subordinated to effects of lyric quality. There are numerous instances of "action" and "history" in each of the volumes, but their accumulation and their unfolding follow what may be the theory of unanimism in that they do not stand for significance in themselves but for some larger motive which rules their destiny. We follow action and history in *Les Hommes de Bonne Volonté* as we follow symbol or allegory. The daily tritenesses of so many men of good will shift our attention to the clarity with which they are narrated, to their color and their speed, to the very form which they take in adhering one to another, like the various layers of a coral island.

There is the lyricism of events and the lyricism of human beings; of the interruptions of events and of the vacillation of human beings. And all these forms of lyricism are spoken without much difference of tone, because all men are joined by their common good will, and a simple act of any one of them is known and understood by all. The lyricism of Romains states that no single act is important in itself, but whether or not it is felt by the group is important. He has chosen the lyricism of a period in history of great upheaval: "Nous sommes dans un temps qui semble encore promis à de fortes secousses, qui semble même les appeler . . ."

(vol. 19, p. 168.) and the lyricism of war fills some of his most moving pages.

Constantly throughout the work is heard the lyricism of Paris: the noises in the rue Réaumur (vol. 3); the *Closerie des Lilas* and the meeting of poets (vol. 4); little Louis Bastide selling his bags of coffee (vol. 6); the industrial landscape: pages in which Romains equals the lyricism of Zola and Verhaeren (vol. 9). The strong abundant lyricism of the city cuts across many of the pages in the twentieth volume. The vision of poverty-stricken Odessa of 1922 incites in Jallez humanitarian and philosophical thoughts. In this new volume observations on our period as a whole become more and more important: the degradation of our world was announced by the first World War and since that time, like some gigantic forest fire, one part after another has been caught in the general conflagration. "La guerre a été la trompette du sabbat. Depuis, tout se peut, tout se voit, tout revient." (Vol. 20, p. 292.)

But the adventure of man is eternal, believes Jallez. And the earth itself covers his adventure. The vastness of this new literary work is like the vastness of the new Russia which Jallez discovers. It is an endless land which man needs for his endless adventure. "Sire, tout est dans le caractère français," Maykosen says to William II (vol. 15, p. 214), and one feels that in his novel Jules Romains is attempting to describe the drama of modern humanity as it operates on the French character and the French nation. France will be the most lucid sufferer of the modern tragedy. It would seem that M. Romains believes this tragedy to be the impotency of the multitudes to use the liberty which they had acquired. The men of good will of our century enter life as dancers enter a round which has been opened up for them and dance mechanically and unnaturally. What can be the future, if they persist in using only the normal and reasonable means for the mastery of events?

THE WORLD OF PROUST AND
SHAKESPEARE

THE TRAGIC HERO has deserted tragedy and crept into the novel. His destiny has discovered here more space for his action and for his suffering. Always, tragedy has been prepared by the world making itself felt in the virtue and vice of a solitary man. More elaborately than any other literary artist, Marcel Proust prepared the setting for tragedy and the actors who seemed destined to portray tragedy. But this longest preparation in art never ceased being just that. Proust contemplated tragedy throughout the composition of his thousands of pages; he never lived it.

The heroes of Proust, because of their unreciprocated love, are, more than other heroes in literature, the great solitary ones. Like a violently lighted room, each hero: Swann, Charlus, Marcel, absorbs in himself a world of cruel light and the rest of the house, the other beings and the other décors, disappears in darkness.

The jealousy of Swann for Odette is a shadow which follows his love everywhere. Odette is the mistress under suspicion when she is absent, when she is present, even when perhaps she is no longer loved. Swann caresses and cradles all the insignificant words of Odette and also all those which she never uttered. The joy of Swann, of which he is surest, is his cohabitation with the absent Odette. There he is all powerful and his very jealousy can change into voluptuousness. Surrounded by friends or alone, he thinks of her and this thought leaps on to his knees and cuddles down

79

"comme une bête aimée qu'on emmène partout et qu'il garderait avec lui, à table, à l'insu des convives."

Swann is the hero who loves. But the classical hero usually is the one who is loved. Hamlet, for example. Hamlet represents the type of hero who is jealous of his fate as a man and not of his fate as a lover. Rodrigue also. Even Othello, blindest of them all, knows constantly that he is loved by Desdemona. But Swann, antithesis of the classical hero, no longer feels the world living around him. He is the world itself before which he must make his mistress kneel down. Hamlet, before he can enjoy his love (which remains intact throughout the duration of the work), must make the world kneel down before his human pride. It is true that Hamlet's action in the world is clear: revenge for murder and revindication of maternal love. Swann's action in the world is diffuse. It is not a world he inhabits, it is a worldliness. Hamlet breathes deeply while he raises a man up to the measurement of tragedy. The prince becomes a hero because he surpasses himself and because he explores a mystery exterior to himself. Swann stifles and sobs in his effort to diminish a tragedy in order to meet the measurement of a man. The one mystery in his life is his own heart.

If the heart of Swann vows to Odette a sentiment of veneration, his intelligence—however lucid it may be in most details—is unable to comprehend the principal fact that Odette is a "cocotte." Swann knows it, but he refuses to know the action of this fact on his life. We see Swann, throughout the long novel of Proust and especially in the first part, only when his nature is attenuated. He demands that Odette pay him the homage of admiration and gratitude, knowing all the time that she is forever incapable of seizing the complexity of his tastes and his tenderness. However, the studious life of an artist, which Swann has always led, discovers its true function in his love. The woman, at the moments when she is the most loved, remains indifferent and cold like an object of art, but makes suffer and exist the sensibility of her lover which until then had been meticulously prepared to suffer and exist. The lover is no longer the man. His nature is changed, because suddenly it has found itself attached to a new experience. And Swann does not dominate this experience as he had always dominated aesthetic experiences, he undergoes it.

The theory of love developed by Swann appears precisely the opposite of the one dear to the Provençal poets and Dante. For these, the mistress symbolizes the light of truth. Love is the new faculty susceptible of leading the lover toward all the perfections, toward God Himself. Swann also considers love an intellectual pleasure, but the object of his love remains exclusively a woman and never becomes a symbol of virtue. The light of truth flows from Beatrice, but the light of truth which Swann seeks (and the formula is in Proust), is that which concerns the actions, the projects, and the past of Odette. The world of Beatrice, apogee of Dante's voyage, is Paradise. The world of Ophelia is that purity of which Hamlet must make himself worthy before contemplating it. The world of Odette, composed of places vaguely known by Swann but which he would like to explore in order to suffer there, is the demimonde of facile fidelities. From a purely psychological viewpoint, Swann is the intellectual and Odette is the instinctive type. Proust the artist is curious to study and understand a temperament opposed to his own which is capable of living immediately in the world and enjoying the moment Swann is the initial representation of Marcel, whose drama is not essentially that of love. It is the drama which recaptures certain moments when love had been apprehended sensorially and when, by that very fact, the tragedy and dissolution of such a love became as real as the experience which was being lived. The future for Hamlet remains always the future, and his tragedy occurs at the end of the play. But in the episode, "Un Amour de Swann," the future is constantly becoming the past, because the tragedy is known, accepted and experienced throughout the inner action of Swann's self-analysis. In Shakespeare, a character gradually develops into the hero and at the end, assumes the burden of the tragedy. In Proust, the hero makes countless efforts to diminish his stature into that of a man and thus to live and to feel like a man. He is tragic at the outset and tries to disburden himself of that honor.

Pride is the constant and implacable corollary of love for Swann. In his agitation, which at times resembles almost a kind of witchcraft dance (the night wanderings of Swann have a curious magical glow about them), his taste becomes increasingly exclusive. A taste dedicated to one principle. The taste of a witch doctor, a priest, a hierophant. The need to possess Odette is the rite of this religion. And, as in all religions which remain active, this need is insensate and profound. Swann's taste, which in our analogy becomes a kind of religious doctrine unaffected by time, represents his point of honor, his "glory" as the seventeenth century would have called it. So imperious is this taste—because, of course, all his life had been dedicated to its development and fulfillment—that when he knows it cannot be satisfied —that is, in looking for Odette one night—he continues a futile search because it would be cruel to renounce the search.

Odette incarnates Swann's love for beauty, and his pride is wounded because he knows that Odette's particular beauty will not last. "L'amour a tellement besoin de se trouver une garantie de durée." The element of pride in Swann's love grows to such proportions that it ends by taking on a kind of responsibility. It ends by remaining alone. Proust recaptures time by effecting three transformations or three replacements: the hero yields to his pride; the lover yields to his love; the artist yields to his work.

Aschenbach, in Thomas Mann's *Death in Venice*, is a purer type of artist than Swann, but he too is characterized by pride in his reputation and accomplishments. Aschenbach never becomes the prisoner of his pride, as Swann does; he is prisoner of his work. Neither man ever knew the facile liberty of normal living. They are voluptuaries of art. "Art is a heightened mode of existence," we read in the Mann story. Natural voluptuousness for most men is intermittent and passing. For Swann and Aschenbach, voluptuousness is an everlasting gaoler. The pride of the connaisseur is the love of the most faithful lover imaginable. He is the lover who will forever see himself and his particular apprehension of beauty in his past love or in any new depiction of it: Aschenbach watching Tadzio on the beach, and Swann looking at Odette in the salon of Mme. Verdurin.

For Swann, then, love is the product of his taste in art, behind which and before which stretches indomitably the connaisseur's pride. His love is never pure because of this rich ingredient of pride and because of his particular form of suffering. This suffering, born from jealousy, seems to emerge from Swann's lack of knowledge about Odette. He would cease suffering if he could know all.

It is true that Proust is no metaphysician. He is an artist. But his hero's problem is epistemological in nature. The studious life of Swann had taught him that the search of the connaisseur is the search for facts. This habit he maintains in his rôle of lover. The search of the lover is the search for facts. And now the derisive tragedy becomes clearer. Whereas the facts about a painting are stable, those which concern human beings and human life are changing facts often shrouded in incomprehensible mystery. Swann is predestined to suffering by his temperament and by the too neat transformation he undergoes from aesthete into lover.

There is an interesting resemblance between Swann and the Provençal poets (and those of the *dolce stil nuovo*) in the distance they feel exists between them and the object loved. But with the poets of the south, this distance is suitable to the tone of worship in their love. They worship the impeccable woman, the spiritual mistress. Not only is Swann's world naturally remote from Odette's, but he increases the separation by the morbidity of his imaginings. Daily he invents evil designs to explain Odette's conduct. In this evolution of the hero-lover, the sick man should be raised to health by love. This is Dante's testimonial, and Cavalcanti's. But in Proust's work the artist is overcome by a peculiar suffering which is a malady. Swann frankly faces the nature of this malady when he realizes that to cease being suspicious of Odette would be to cease loving her. Swann accepts the impossibility of any cure. His is the cherished malady. To be cured would be to die.

Hamlet seeks knowledge which will permit him to act.

But Swann, refusing to act and thereby cause his spell to vanish, invents false facts in order to maintain his fever. The modern hero in literature seems to be characterized by his search and effort to adjust the world to the facts of his imagination. Thus, the modern hero represents, to an extraordinary degree, a case of infantilism. He is a child, not because of his innocency, but by his reconstruction of a distorted world. Hamlet, the type of classical hero, strives in the opposite direction. His action is not self-protective and remote from reality. It is a piercing of all that has obscured his mind from the understanding of reality. To live, for Hamlet, becomes equivalent to leaving his books, his childhood, his traditions, and testing their maturing power on what the world inevitably provides of deceit, lust, mercy. Hamlet goes into a world he doesn't know, where he will have to readjust his vision and his strength. Shakespeare's art is the art of the world to be conquered.

Proust's art is the art of the world to be remembered. Swann is the hero when he remembers, thanks to the sound of music, the figure of Odette flanked by the Verdurins and the Cottards. His world is reenacted by a violent and subversive memory, the richest perhaps in all literature. But the hero condenses the world into a salon and the salon into his fever. This he will not leave, because there is nothing outside of it. Neither will Aschenbach leave Venice. Fever-infested Venice is the symbol in Mann's story for the world of the modern hero who seeks his death, wilfully, in all that is unreal to himself. "Something is rotten in the state of Denmark" is not a modern ejaculation.

The mind of the hero has become the mind of the artist, who, having learned the strange power that can be exerted over all that he creates, has been confounded by the power which the real world seeks to exert over him. To escape this dilemma, which is simple and habitual, he has constructed a more complicated one in his effort to consider the world, an art, and human struggle in the world, the artistic creation.

As Swann listens to the brief recurring theme in Vinteuil's sonata, with which he has come to associate his love for Odette, he feels the proportions of his soul change. In himself the hero has learned how to liberate a space necessary for the action and the movement of his memory. In contradiction with the hero who is forced to compose his action in the present-invading-future, Swann is the hero of the present-invading-past. The world enters into him as if it had no more consistency than the sounds of Vinteuil's music have in the air. The world is malleable. It is subtilized by some lyric chemistry, even as the will of the hero has subtilized evil.

Later in the work, there is another metaphor, another delicate notation concerning the musical motifs in Vinteuil's sonata. The motifs become for Swann ideas which fill the great unpenetrated night of his soul. ("qui remplissent la grande nuit impénétrée de son âme.") This is an extraordinary adjective, *impénétrée*, which bears in it the paradox of Proust's entire novel, and more particularly, the paradox of Swann's love. Proust is saying that musical motifs, like ideas, are *filling* the soul of his hero which is *unpenetrated*. This seems to be equivalent to saying that the hero is filling his memory with the unreal furnishings of memory. The active hero usually heeds a contrary supplication: the great necessity for the soul to empty itself and thereby to face the present and to prepare the future.

This paradox of metaphor leads us back to the paradox

of morals. Soon after Proust completes the image of
Swann's 'love being a malady' by having his hero say that
his love cannot be operated on ("son mal n'est plus op-
érable"), Swann realizes that Odette's real sentiment of
love for him is over. He continues, however, to listen to
Vinteuil's music, which is endowed for him more and more
with a supernatural prestige. He enters the final phase of
his love, when absolute immobility of his being is required
for the recapture of his love—that is, for the perfect hearing of musical themes which have assumed the sentiment
of his love.

Swann becomes finally, then, the lover of beauty who is
unable to possess it. As Aschenbach is the creator of beauty
who is unable to possess it. Both, through this incapacity
to possess what they love, stand for a new type of hero.
Swann is the modern hero whose action has become contemplation. (5) Odette is in reality no woman at all for
Swann; she is a painting of Botticelli. Likewise, Tadzio, in
the rich and poignant imagination of Aschenbach, is the
smile of Narcissus.

One of the great moments in Hamlet's struggle is when
he makes this extraordinary request of his mother: "For-
give me this my virtue." Hamlet is the innocent who wills
the action of virtue and whose tragedy occurs when the
power opposed to virtue prevails. Today, in Swann and
Aschenbach, for example, the hero has reversed this extraordinary request of a son to his mother, and utters its
equally extraordinary opposite: "Grant me this my vice."
This request the modern hero doesn't make to his mother
(who in Hamlet's case represented the hero's world), but
he makes it to himself!

The old adage of Socrates, "Know thyself," is certainly

at the core of every heroic deed and of every effort toward the achievement of heroism. But today, the heroism of knowing oneself has become the heroism of not knowing oneself, or rather the heroism of flight from all that is central in oneself. The modern hero's heart is the heart fluctuating. Proust's phrase, "les intermittences du coeur," which he at one time destined for the general title of his work, is the key phrase for modern psychology. And psychologism, I fully believe, will characterize our age (if anything remains after the wars of our age) as humanism characterizes the Renaissance and as scholasticism characterizes the Middle Ages.

The "intermittences of the heart" is the phrase in which converge the profoundest meanings of romanticism and scepticism. Romanticism is the study of the self that is not central in man; I am almost prepared to say that it is the study of the non-existent self. (The so-called romanticism of Corneille's *Cid* is not the romanticism of Marcel Proust's novel.) Scepticism is the belief that a man is equally composed of a positive self and a negative one. With this belief, the self never really is; it is always becoming.

Out of a romanticism of valor and love striving to harmonize with the world and thereby purify it—that is, out of the romanticism of *Le Cid* and *Hamlet*, has been forged the romanticism of self-analysis and self-pity. Out of the scepticism of the Renaissance, that is, the scepticism of Montaigne and Hamlet, which was doubt arising from an absence of facts and a wonderment over the meaning of an isolated fact and its mobile meaning arising from its juxtaposition with other facts, has grown the modern scepticism concerning truth and values.

Tragedy does not arise from the intermittences of a

hero's heart. It arises from the hero's pact made with the world; a pact that is unremitting and sealed. Tragedy follows contemplation because tragedy is a commitment. (In contemplation there is no need for commitment.) Proust's hero contemplates the world of his sensitivity and signs no pact with any other world. He knows all the dangerous freedom of intermittences and ignores the danger of a willed subservience. Swann does not live in alliance with his destiny. He lives in the dissolution of all his moral prejudices and he seeks no escape from this empty state. He is the contemplator of infecundity and the modern hero of inaction.

Part III
THE POET'S CREATION

CHARLES BAUDELAIRE:
The Experience of Religious Heroism

Introduction

BAUDELAIRE is the modern hero who inhabits solitude.
Before him, *literary* heroes didn't live in solitude: Oedipus
didn't, nor did Macbeth, nor Rodrigue. Hamlet first announced the new climate which the modern hero was destined to know. But there is a vast difference between Hamlet's solitude and Baudelaire's! (We have the right to list
together a tragic hero and a poet because the great tragic
books of the nineteenth and twentieth centuries are auto-
biographies: *Les Fleurs du Mal, Une Saison en Enfer,
Ulysses, A la recherche du temps perdu, Nightwood,* and
the modern writer does not conceal from his reader the bitter solitude which the work itself is for him, the very work
which he feels impelled to write with the sentiment of
fatality which forced Oedipus and Macbeth to accomplish
their destiny of action.)

When compared with Baudelaire's, other forms of modern solitude appear less cruel and less desperate; his alone
is without affection and without labor. It was emptied of all
that can make human solitude glorious and enriching.
Baudelaire did not even have the memory of happiness in
his solitude, nor its hope. He had only his mother, who
lived away from him and never understood her son. "Je
crois vraiment, ma chère mère, que vous n'avez jamais
connu mon insupportable sensibilité." (*Lettres à sa mère,*

93

p. 118.) Baudelaire's mother was incapable of understanding the two realities which counted the most for the poet:
his child's heart and the seriousness of his writing which he
tried all his life to prove to her. What was truest for
Baudelaire was his heart—so densely populated and so
troubled that the poet had no need to invent beings; his
heart was all beings, all gardens, all peoples, all disasters.
What was most precious for Baudelaire was his papers, his
manuscripts, his books. If books are contemplated long
enough, they can become as human as landscapes. Neither
the heart nor the books of Charles Baudelaire were known
to his mother, Caroline. She would send him reproaches,
money, tender messages. And in his letters to his mother
he would tell her above all how hounded he was for pay-
ments on debts and how he had sunk into periods of de-
pression which had interrupted all work. Baudelaire never
found much space in his letters to Caroline for affection,
and yet he knew that his cure would come about only
through affection and love.

Modern literature deals essentially with childhood and
adolescence (cf. *Les Fleurs du Mal* of Baudelaire, *Les
Faux-Monnayeurs* of Gide, *Portrait of the Artist as Young
Man* of Joyce, *Du Côté de chez Swann* of Proust, *Death of
the Heart* of Elizabeth Bowen, the novels of Mauriac) because the modern hero never ceases measuring the universe
with his own heart. This is the habit and pride of children.
The child very naturally loves his mother and she can represent the universe for him since she was in a literal sense
his universe during the first months of his existence. But if
maternal love persists in man as his deepest and most powerful force (Oedipus, Hamlet, Proust, Baudelaire), the
world remains always the child's world, reduced and con-

tained within the limits of a single heart. Many modern
heroes, if they are without the complex of maternal love,
love a woman filially and try to discover passively in her
their universe. (cf. Julien in *Le Rouge et le Noir* of Stend-
hal, Jérôme in *La Porte Etroite* of Gide, Constantine in
the *Sea Gull* of Chekhov.)

Baudelaire's greatness is his book. His greatness is the sinister cold beauty he created. *Les Fleurs du Mal* is a book
made with the fury of a child and the patience of an artist.
One may pity all the romantic poets of the nineteenth century, nightingales whose song is measureless. But one can
be afraid of Charles Baudelaire. He was very far from his
contemporaries: Gautier, Hugo, Leconte de Lisle. He was
very near Villon. (As Mauriac is today very far from his
contemporaries: D. H. Lawrence, Duhamel, Romains—
and remains very near Racine.) Great poets, like great
books, propagate one another. Baudelaire welcomed, in the
midst of nineteenth century ruins, the true state of man.

The spirit of man is submitted to incessant metamor-
phoses and it is true that Baudelaire's book teaches that
happiness is essentially what does not last. But the Christian spirit receives a special mark which is as clearly visible
in *Les Fleurs du Mal* as in St. Augustine's *Confessions*.
Christian thought possesses itself and never leaves itself.
Baudelaire's solitude is filled and penetrated. It is the solitude of an exile who keeps the memory of a distant voyage
he has never taken.

"Là, tout n'est qu'ordre et beauté."

The Christian cannot forget his life. He cannot forget his
childhood, or his adolescence, or yesterday. This transcendent
memory appears in any great art, but especially, perhaps,

in the most finished pages of personal lyricism. Prose is a resurrection of life; poetry is another life, charged with another meaning and a new value. Whereas a novel is the hope of survival, a poem is an autonomous and distinct life. Prose reflects the attacks made on a human being and the modifications he *underwent*. But poetry translates the memory of the attacks which the human being *sustained* against the world.

Les Fleurs du Mal is therefore a book of human courage and, moreover, a book of chastity. Readers today are becoming more aware of these two values of Baudelaire. His courage is his moment in history, the precise moment in the centuries when Baudelaire looked at "les nations corrompues" and "le dieu de l'Utile" (cf. "J'aime le souvenir de ces époques nues." *Les Fleurs du Mal*, V.) His chastity is his knowledge that one must desire the good even with an impoverished will. His passion attained the same purity of the great idealistic poets: Dante, Cavalcanti, Petrarch, but with more clairvoyance. The specifically French sign of passion is the clairvoyance of the heart which accompanies it.

Baudelaire's lyric humanism unquestionably played an important part in the creation of the epic humanism of Proust and Joyce. The richness and coherence of the Middle Ages will perhaps return. But the new order, as we are able to distinguish it today through the smoke and noise of war, has not yet gone beyond the search for order.

We like to consider Baudelaire's malady an incapacity to approach the good, the result of that myth of the modern age that man no longer needs God. But Baudelaire did not hesitate to proclaim that sin is a deicide. The ransom of the genius is heavy, heavier for Baudelaire and the modern

artist than for Dante and Pascal. His terrible lucidity about
the ransom explains why Baudelaire became one of the
greatest critics of all time. His criticism is his real renovation because it is his psychological and theological knowledge, his understanding of man's reality.

The Man

In the cemetery of Montparnasse, Baudelaire's monument, sculptured by the artist Charmoy, who was to die
soon after the work was completed, represents the life-
sized figure of the poet wrapped in funereal cloth and lying
on a slab of stone. Only the face is revealed. The features
in grey stone reflect repose and quietude, a deathlike immobility. Although the eyes are closed, the sculptor has
caught an expression which resembles that of contemplation. Baudelaire is looking inwardly. His attention is fixed
upon a mystery which has been unfolded. A slender column
rises into the air at the head of the stone slab. On this
column is a head resting in the palms of two hands. Life is
carved on this stone, a life of malediction. The harsh features of this spirit of evil, with eyes opened, are also in an
attitude of contemplation, intent upon some undefined
object directly ahead. These eyes of evil are looking out
over the body of Baudelaire who is lost in an inner delectation. The significance of Baudelaire's poetry is thus translated by the sculptor. The essence of *Les Fleurs du Mal*
was extracted from a spiritual experience. The adornment
of this poetry and its generative power came from what the
Church defines as sin. Baudelaire also defined it as sin. The
more intimately he knew it, the more apprehensive he
became about the spiritual life of man. Like the dual vision
of the Montparnasse monument, there was a Baudelaire

who derived from his contemplation of horror and evil a desire to behold the mystery of his transgressions.

The poet succinctly describes his youth as a "dark storm" (*un ténébreux orage*). His high-pitched sentiments vacillated between an inordinate love for his mother, which unquestionably had as a basis an erotic impulse, and a hatred for his step-father, which resembled a lover's jealousy. As he passed from a fiery adolescence into early manhood, his two-fold nature of lethargy and anger developed proportionately. Baudelaire became the "dandy," the independent critic and artist who has received his family's patrimony, and at the same time the rebel, the defier of bourgeois conventionality. Endowed with a super-sensitiveness and hampered by an incapacity to accept any of the trials of existence, he never overcame the innate acedia which alternated with exasperation. Baudelaire's literary testament is a union of sensibility and malady. The sensibility is spiritual and the malady is sensorial.

On the small island behind the cathedral, l'Ile Saint Louis, on the third floor of the stately seventeenth century Hôtel Lauzun, Baudelaire painfully distilled verses sombre like the very façade of the house and grey like the parapets on the river bank. All the shades between white and black, all the shades of the Paris fog, all the shades between his two favorite words: "livid" and "tenebrific," cover the canvas on which the painted flowers imitate life not by their colors but by their multiple perfumes. (6) Between walls which reverberated with the bells of Notre Dame, Baudelaire sought a sensual release in the arms of his mistress, Jeanne Duval, and fought the implacable usurer. The dark skin of Jeanne, the "Vénus noire," was another tone in the scale, another note added to the night of Baudelaire's Hope and Despair, another reflection in the waters of the Seine which surrounded him. The courtesan, the money-lender, the city's greyness are the subordinate actors to the principal character, Baudelaire's malady which he names "spleen." This spleen was a spiritual debauchery, graver than carnal sin. It was the tragic element in Baudelaire's drama because it seemed to grow stronger as he became more conscious of it.

The proof of this spleen's tenacity is in a work written after *Les Fleurs du Mal,* which bears the inscription, *Mon Cœur mis à nu.* The title was suggested by a title in Poe's *Marginalia,* "My heart laid bare." This intimate journal of Baudelaire vibrates with his varied problems. It expresses his hatreds and his bitterness, but it also reveals a heart humbled before the spiritual heritage of humanity. As acutely as in his poetry, Baudelaire says in summary: Here is a man impoverished by his weaknesses; a man whose experience leads him to say that "love is the taste for prostitution" and yet who knows that there is another love whose object is a muse and whose rite is contemplation; a man who would work and who cannot and whose empty past horrifies his fruitless present.

The image of the sea returns frequently in Baudelaire's poetry. His direct experience with the sea, the voyage to l'Ile Maurice, was both an exile, brought about by his stepfather, and a liberation from a presence which incensed him. When the image recurs, he symbolizes in it his dual obsession, his "spleen" and his "idéal." In the ocean's breadth, in its darkness, in its tumult, "le rire énorme de la mer" as he calls it, he discovers his own mind and his conquered will. There is a correspondence between the tormented waves and the restless heart. Yet this same vastness of the sea and the mystery of unplumbed depths are, in the poetic image, the heart consoled, the triumph of strife and effort. The sea is not a destructive force, but it is a calm berceuse. That is why the poet at moments when he is nearest his "idéal," when he is listening to music, for example, compares the effect of music to the effect of the sea:

La musique souvent me prend comme une mer!

Both music and the sea can transport the poet to a climate where his spleen is inaccessible.

The Artist

In the history of nineteenth century French poetry Baudelaire occupies a double place as announcer; on the one hand, as announcer of a spiritual restlessness which will be treated presently in this essay, and on the other hand as announcer of a new poetic preoccupation. It is difficult to dissociate the art of Baudelaire's poetry from the poet's experience. One engenders the other. The experience itself is not narrated however, but a "state" resulting from emotion or shock is transcribed. The transcription is the essence of what is most vacillating and most ineffable: a spiritual communication. The means used to produce this transcription are the most universal sensorial experiences of man apt to evoke or connote the particular personal experience of the poet. In this way the unique becomes the multiple, the unfathomable becomes the revealed.

The facile lyric flow of Hugo, whose best volumes of verse were contemporary with *Les Fleurs du Mal*, was distasteful to Baudelaire. Perhaps not so distasteful as untrue. There is nothing in Baudelaire's volume that resembles the chronicle form so lavishly employed by Hugo. It was Poe whom Baudelaire called his "brother" and whose *Poetic Principle* left such an intense impression on the French poet. In this literary discovery, as well as in the artistic discoveries of Delacroix and Manet and the musical discovery of Wagner, Baudelaire subsumes the lesson he appropriates. The completeness of his artistic understanding enables him to utilize the form, the color, the sound. These channels to a truer poetic state he imposes upon the poets who follow him: Verlaine, Rimbaud, Mallarmé. In their work the "channels" occupy so important a place that the emotional excitement which brought the poem into being is often completely obscured. But in Baudelaire it palpitates with unashamed reality.

The spectacle of the exterior world exists for Baudelaire only in so far as it reflects the spectacle of an inner peace or an inner disquietude. Both of these spectacles, the one materialistic and the other immaterial, are dark and discreet, guardians of strange secrets. Man, or more exactly the poet, builds his existence on the double rhythm of exploring the spectacle of life and the spectacle of himself. Both are fortresses impossible of capture in any ordinary manner. Both require a mystical approach. Nature is a temple. The poet enters it as if he were entering the holy place of symbols. The poetic experience at this precise moment is made up of a profound unity. It is then that the poet perceives the analogy, dear to Swedenborg, that exists between heaven and earth. An expansion operates in the poet's being which indicates that the experience is akin to a mystical experience.

Baudelaire as the artist eternally seeking unity, analogy, precision, is the poet of the short poem and, indeed, the artist of the single line. The image condensed, at times brutally explosive, harmonizes with the intense poetic state

so difficult of attainment and so prone to vanish. In a single
line the poet describes his longing, unsatiated, for his mistress: desires which go toward her in caravan fashion
("Quand vers toi mes désirs partent en caravane.") It is an
admirable image which paints the painfully slow journey of
love toward its satisfaction. In another poem where Baudelaire describes the elaborate altar he wishes to erect to
his mistress, he tells her that his thoughts will be drawn
up as candles: "Tu verras mes Pensers, rangés comme des
cierges," and thus symbolizes the flames which burn in an
act of adoration.

If the imagery isn't striking in some of the poems, the
musical element and the purely sensual vitality dominate.
Le Balcon, for example, without condensing any images,
except in one of its thirty lines, fuses various sentiments
and evocations into a unified state. The setting sun and the
warmth of the fire indicate that perishing light has called
into the poet's mind the concept of imperishable love. Over
this scene night thickens like a wall (it is the line of the
condensed image) and with the darkness an indescribable
sensuality invades the lovers:

> La nuit s'épaississait ainsi qu'une cloison,
> Et mes yeux dans le noir devinaient tes prunelles,
> Et je buvais ton souffle, ô douceur! ô poison!
> Et tes pieds s'endormaient dans mes mains fraternelles.
> La nuit s'épaississait ainsi qu'une cloison.

The domain of sensuality finally broadens out into infini-
tude. The escape the lovers had sought ends in a spiritual
frustration. It is (in the second line of the last stanza) the
abyss which they cannot fathom, "un gouffre interdit à nos
sondes." The dream of Baudelaire, evoked in a rare music

of nostalgia, reaches its climax in the mystery of rejuvenation and rebirth. The rhythm of man's happiness is not even or sustained. A crescendo in order to become greater must sink first. *Le Balcon,* which is doubtless a memory of Jeanne Duval, develops the same plan as most of his spiritual pieces. Any approximation to a sense of order implies a previous state of disorder, a spiritualization of love follows the physical experience, an aspiration toward the Good results from a knowledge of Evil.

If the world is, in the words of Baudelaire, a vast system of contradictions, the preoccupation of the artist is to discover order where chaos exists. What is order in the world must of necessity be spiritual. The words themselves "esprit" and "spirituel" are the words most often used by Baudelaire. His art not only announces a conquest of the spiritual; it is the conquest itself. *Les Fleurs du Mal,* as truly as the *Divine Comedy,* and with greater personal anguish than the poem of Dante, is an art which both in its essence and in its adornments is the annunciation of God. One may object that Baudelaire defines Beauty as something ardent and sad, and that Beauty in God should be purity and joy. But a state outside of grace cannot be joyful, and does not exclude belief. Baudelaire, as an artist, is condemned to paint on darkness. But because this art is for him a magic in which he will use formulas of incantation, the darkness is black and yet luminous, "noire et pourtant lumineuse." In his prose writings he claims two literary qualities: supernaturalism and irony. Their commingling is the witchcraft which is the necessary procedure for Baudelaire's communication. Satan has his own beauty in *Les Fleurs du Mal.*

Baudelaire has no illusions about the Demon at his side.

He compares the influence of evil to the air around him. It is interesting to note in this connection that the Jesuit priest, Gerard Manley Hopkins, compares the Virgin to the air we breathe. Baudelaire, the poet of sin, and Father Hopkins, the poet of grace, are both poets whose art is witness to the spiritual. As the psychologist is sometimes tricked into believing he can pierce secrets of the heart which are known only to the confessor and to God, so the artist is deceived by ruses in his art. Vigor in art must come from some mystical nourishment whose source is not poisoned. We have said that Baudelaire seeks to reach a state of poetry. He does this, and very often he does more. The profound experience of his art succeeds in making the state of poetry a poetic state of grace.

De Profundis

Because of the predominance of spirituality in the work of Baudelaire, it is easy to forget that, after all, as far as man can judge, he was blocked off during manhood from God's grace. His poetry is that of a man in agony. He was a visionary who never knew ecstasy. The barrier (to use a favorite word of the mystics) which prevented Baudelaire from seeing more clearly was unquestionably eroticism. His whole treatment of love describes it as a carnal indulgence and complex, a trap set by the spirit of evil for the damnation of man.

If he heard the call of God, it was only confusedly. As a child he was given a careful religious education. It was somewhere during the years 1842 and 1850 that he lost faith in the Catholic Church. But Baudelaire is an excellent proof for a belief the Church has always held; namely, that once a Christian, it is impossible to dispossess oneself of the spirit of Christianity. The sacraments leave an indelible mark. Baudelaire notes that as a child he held conversations with God; later, in the very midst of incredulity, he experienced a need for prayer. In his intimate journal he states beliefs that are at least suggested in his poetry. His theory of true civilization is a startling example. He writes "Théorie de la vraie civilisation. Elle n'est pas dans le gaz, ni dans la vapeur, ni dans les tables tournantes. Elle est dans la diminution des traces du péché originel."

With a power comparable to Dante's, although not so sustained, Baudelaire paints the picture of sin in some of its blackest aspects. Curiously enough in this poetry, sin is rarely pictured without death. It is death in the true Villon style, the physical horror of decomposition. In the passages where love is figured as death, where sin is represented with its reward, Baudelaire echoes both Dante and Villon.

Acedia is the sin which Baudelaire characterizes in his *Journaux Intimes* as the malady of monks. Acedia is also Baudelaire's sin which, coupled with eroticism, made his case one of the most hopeless. A lustful desire, if it exists by itself, may be conquered by exercise of the will. Acedia is precisely the sin of spiritual indolence. It springs from a paucity of spiritual desire. Not concerned with belief, it prevents the believer from demonstrating actively the tenets of his faith. Dante places acedia in one of his least chastised circles, but for Baudelaire it was the "spleen," the spiritual impotency, which was at the base of his cerebral suffering.

In a sonnet to which he gave as a title the Biblical phrase, *De Profundis Clamavi*, Baudelaire synthesizes the major themes in *Les Fleurs du Mal*: his own tragic experience of twenty years, the spectacle of the universe which remains in his memory as a dull grey horizon (he uses another favorite word: "l'horizon plombé") and, more precisely, the night of his disorder:

> Et cette immense nuit semblable au vieux chaos.

There is at the beginning of these fourteen lines one which, from the religious viewpoint, is the most important Baudelaire composed. In it he implores God's pity and states that God is the only one he truly loves:

> J'implore ta pitié, Toi, l'unique que j'aime.

The whole sonnet is worthy of a mystic who has known the world and who has renounced it, a Jacopone da Todi or a Saint Augustine. It is the confession of a man who has experienced in the flesh the death of himself. The remarkable part of the piece is that it doesn't treat a pure pessimism, a pessimism like de Vigny's for example, which would reject all existence. Baudelaire's pessimism is mitigated by his understanding of it and by his prayer for aid. Even in the poems which are blasphemous, the poems of Baudelaire's so-called "satanism," his belief in Satan presupposes a belief in God. T. S. Eliot, in his essay on Baudelaire, states that "genuine blasphemy is the product of partial belief."

As day follows night, the sinner can behold a spiritual dawn. Baudelaire seemed to require extreme debauchery in order to feel afterwards the need of purification. He would experience voluptuousness only when he would be conscious of sinning. He has recorded that after sin he experienced a great thirst for purity and beauty. This he calls an avenging mystery. In the brute an angel awakens. In addition to the courtesan type, Jeanne Duval, there was in the life of Baudelaire the muse, Madame Sabatier, who awakened in him the chivalric form of love. He approaches her only in trembling. It is thoughts of her that awaken the angel. She is the goddess whose image he evokes in his mind after the "stupid orgies" (as he calls them) which exhaust him.

I dare say that the most profound spiritual lesson which Baudelaire underwent was the sudden craving for contact with what he characterizes as the "resplendent soul" of his goddess. The moment he felt remorse and hope coincided with disgust for sin. This is a mystical experience which has been recorded in the narratives of countless conversions. When Baudelaire comments on the art of Daumier, he expresses a truth about his own work. The artist has used satire and mockery in depicting the spirit of evil in the world, but in the very energy and sincerity of his conception of evil, he has revealed the beauty of his heart. His laughter is impure: it has an element of horror. His ribaldry is impure: it has an element of disgust.

Conclusion

The poet, more lucidly than other artists, reflects the dual nature of man. The poetry of Baudelaire, like that of Villon and of Racine, is a precise testimonial to the vast antithesis (7) in our characters between good and evil. Our heritage is the capacity to choose. It would seem to be a rule that great poetry has its roots in despair. In order to attain human greatness, man must conquer grief. Because it is in his poetic work, the alchemy of his emotions and struggles, that his grief is revealed triumphant or conquered or quasi-conquered, this work has a greater reality than his life. The poet's communication subsumes his biog-

raphy and frequently contradicts it. It is of little conse-
quence if the details of a poet's life are modified or are
lacking in his work, provided he transcribe the journey of
his soul to its source, no matter how far from the source
the soul arrives. The poet becomes a hero only as he becomes the hero of his conscience.

In the cases of both Baudelaire and Racine, we can see
a man convinced of a reality greater than himself and, at
the same time, of a man who, after touching eternity and
recognizing it to be such, lost his grasp on it. Their unhappi-
ness lay in the intermittence of the pure vision which they
knew existed beyond the cloud of worldliness. They knew
that virtue is of a sterner force than vice and one that is
infinitely harder to acquire. What is noble in them, what
makes them heroes of a kind, is that they were completely
lacking in any spiritual indulgence for themselves. They
were not capable of living alone because they were not
saints. And yet the important problems in their lives were
spiritual problems. They were not saints, but they were
poets. Their poetry took the place of prayer and their state
as artists took the place of sainthood.

Villon's religious belief was more vital and more tenacious than Baudelaire's; and his poetic production is ac-
cordingly more subordinate to his spiritual life than Baudelaire's is to his spiritual life. Villon's misdeeds were
innumerable, but his mother (8) could expiate them for
him. According to the mysterious doctrine of the Com-
munion of Saints, a pious act of one individual can alleviate
the sin of another. Baudelaire was more alone. And then
again, Villon was nearer the Christian ideal of humility.
Poverty is a healthful state for the smallest spiritual bless-

ings to survive. The prodigality of Baudelaire was a major impediment of habit. Villon had no opportunity of drowsing off into a dream of false greatness. He never knew the insolence of success. Racine was undermined by flattery and was irascible over other contemporary successes. Baudelaire had not a little in him of the romantic conception of genius, the feeling of isolated and misunderstood greatness. (9) The ordinary result of success is inebriation and not humility. Villon seems far from the type of the professional writer, the artist who produces for a public whom he doesn't know. The obscurity today of his life explains the obscurity of some of his poetry. Those lines which are understood today live because of their spiritual fervor. Maître Villon had much traffic with the world. Maître Villon became a poet when he separated himself from the world in order to see it.

It is more difficult in the case of Racine, the supreme classic artist, to disengage from the setting of Greek mythology and Roman history his personal spiritual problems. Corneille is a more direct poet with his constant glorification of heroism. The noble, the superhuman, the honorable vie for first place in characters in whom nothing low resides. But in the world which Racine created, how many of the characters are motivated and tortured by traits which are the most reprehensible, the most lamentably human! Corneille's characters become greater as that which opposes them grows. The characters of Racine become increasingly human as they remain estranged from any supernatural aid. In the great tragedy of the Christian martyr, *Polyeucte*, Corneille is one of the rare poets who, in dramatic poetry, have succeeded in portraying grace as the irresistible and perfect force. Racine, in his tragedy *Phèdre,* does precisely the opposite in portraying the disorder which ensues from the absence of grace.

There is no detail of Racine's personality in his poetry and yet all his personality is in it. (10) If Racine is the classic and Baudelaire the romantic, the terms can be used only to designate that which is superficial in form and material. Whether the work be called *Phèdre* or *Manfred* or *Les Fleurs du Mal,* there is only one method for the poet to explore any of the spiritual mysteries of man, and that method is an exploration of himself. (11) The result may be couched in a form more universal than personal, more objective than subjective, but after the exchange of terms is made, the value remains the same. Racine's poetry was composed for a court bepowdered and bewigged, where artifice mingled with artificiality, where art was adorned with distant names and painted horizons, but where the essence of human problems strangely resembles that of *Genesis* and of André Gide!

The irony of Baudelaire, which is absent only from his most elevated pieces, is never the sign of spiritual raillery; it is rather the indication of his heart which has not been tricked. Baudelaire unquestionably loved God. But he knew another love which prevented the first from acting. It was his love for the lie. The poet in love with a woman never effaced the man intelligent enough to see through the mask of woman's deceit. Baudelaire knew there were eyes capable of dissembling secrets, that there were jewel boxes without jewels, and that there were medallions without relics. But his perspicacity never prevented him from loving the appearance of beauty. The indifference of a concocted beauty never repulsed him.

It was not only the dichotomy of Baudelaire's loves that engendered his irony and frustration; it was also his search for God within himself. All the Catholic practices imposed upon the faithful are built upon the belief that God is outside of man and that He has to be met in a meeting place. In the words of Suarès: it is God at the rendez-vous who purifies everything. Reason in man must desire God, but the will must act in order to find Him. Reason and Nature are imperfect in themselves. They demand the aid of grace which alone is able to give them supernatural life.

PAUL CLAUDEL:
The Metaphysics of a Poet

I

Paul Claudel appears as the most demanding of contemporary poets. To be understood and followed, he requires from his reader a total spiritual submission and
attention. It is not only the ornate and complex part of his
work which tyrannizes the reader's intelligence, it is above
all the harassing and well-nigh unbearable unity of his
books. This unity provides his reader with no rest, no
dream, no immobility. Claudel hammers in his truth without breathing between the blows. Rightfully considered the
most feared poet, he may also seem the most cruel. And
yet, upon careful examination of his writings, it is impossible to discover precise examples of his cruelty. They give
this general impression because they are unified in their
criticism of the century's spirit. Paradoxically, Claudel is
par excellence the poet of the world, the poet who has
named the greatest number of objects in the world, the
realist poet in his love for the humblest and most familiar
objects; but he is also the most implacably hostile poet to
the superficial world of our century.

The rough harshness of the peasant is in Claudel. He
comes from the Tardenois, a small section of France between the two northern provinces of l'Ile de France and la
Champagne. It is a part of France characterized by agricul-

ture and cathedrals. Claudel as a child saw about him the sowing of the fields and the richness of the earth, and on his horizon the sombre and lasting presence of the cathedrals of Soissons, Laon, Reims. From his childhood he remembers the spectacle, both realist and mystic, which his work testifies to and prolongs, of the earth renewing and recreating itself under the imperious and fecundating silence of the Creator. The act of the sower is like the act of the believer. The earth receives the seed as God receives our love. Later, in time and in eternity, the result and the reward come into being. The tree, one of the most familiar objects on the French landscape and one of the most permanent symbols in Claudel's work, is, like life itself, solidly planted in the earth. Its freedom is its daily slow and sure growth toward the sky. Man is a captive of the earth, but since the earth is God's work, man is therefore the captive of God. He grows up free in a captivity whose limits he will never reach. In one of his books in prose Claudel has written: "Il n'y a pas de paradis sans un arbre, il faut planter quelque chose, c'est le mûrier qui rassemble les vers à soie." His entire work is like a tree growing in all its parts at once, and testifying to a unified strength and inner richness.

At the age of eighteen, in the full sadness and restlessness of eighteen, Claudel discovered Rimbaud. He has described in some detail and with apparent honesty the importance of this spiritual meeting and how he suddenly ceased feeling lonely during his walks along the streets of Paris when he was still a student at the lycée. Claudel acclaimed Rimbaud his guide and initiator and prophet, as Dante had acclaimed Virgil, as Baudelaire had acclaimed Poe. After much studying and reading of poets, Claudel finally came upon a poet who fully felt his responsibility of being, the first who dared to call upon his executioners. Arthur Rimbaud dared to call upon them, because he was still an adolescent when he was a poet, because he still possessed the very pure heroism of adolescence. Claudel discovered in Rimbaud an adolescent at grips with everything that is real, and it was perhaps this feeling of the real, this direct and true vision of things, which is at the source of Claudel's fascination. Rimbaud, the poet of sixteen, who appeared in France in 1870 at a moment of invasion and war, was not a boy like the others, but Claudel knew that Rimbaud's fatality was far from being solely the poet's fatality. Scorn of society, which is a recurrent theme in Rimbaud's *Saison en Enfer,* is less dominant than the theme of his spiritual struggle. Rimbaud makes the effort to bend his will and believe in God. This very effort was the lesson in Rimbaud which Claudel embraced with violence and joy. It was the first important offensive against the spirit of the nineteenth century: reduced to its simplest formula, it taught that art does not guarantee salvation. Claudel learned from the *Illuminations* and from the *Saison en Enfer* that the artist, in his exercises of creator, is not exempt from the responsibilities of creature. His fatality remains the same—that of desiring the good.

Paul Claudel closes, recapitulates, and subsumes the modern movement in poetry. It has often been said that Claudel's poetic power equals Victor Hugo's. This kind of remark reveals a basic misunderstanding of the two poets. Hugo's power is exclusively verbal. It bears no trace of the metaphysical struggle which is the glory and the distinction of modern poetry. And this is why Hugo's power is useless and impotent for men and poets today. Other poets are the real ancestors of Claudel. Baudelaire, for example, is the first who states in a profound way the problem of existence. He takes cognizance of the problem through the fact of evil, its reality, and the suffering it causes. Rimbaud, as we have said, stated the problem of the responsibility of existence. This already represents a progress and development in the spiritual struggle of the modern poet. Mallarmé spoke of another kind of responsibility, that of language and of the object named. He was the artist of the symbol and of the mysterious bonds which attach man to everything that surrounds him. Mallarmé, in a sense, represented Platonic metaphysics, which preceded and prepared Christian metaphysics. He was the master, and his disciple today, M. Paul Valéry, is the thinker who explores and amplifies the lessons of the master.

After Baudelaire, who first stated the basic problem of modern poets; after Mallarmé, who was its master and theorist and whose brief work is a mine of secrets; after Rimbaud, who was its adolescent, that is, the one who underwent the experience in so personal and violent a way that we shall never be able to measure its profundity comes Paul Claudel, whom we make bold to call the "poet." He is a poet in a more vital and more complete sense than these other artists. He is the poet of day who comes after a long line of poets obsessed with night.

The poet is always, in some way or other, Prometheus, thief of fire and the man chained to his rock. These poets of the nineteenth century we have named certainly resembled Prometheus, but they struggled so hard during the night that when day came, they were too exhausted to look at the light. The image of Prometheus applies poorly to Claudel. His own image of the tree is more suitable. A tree is as firmly chained as Prometheus. But its struggle is growth. Day and night it does not cease maturing and realizing itself. The earth, a prison for it, is both favorable and necessary. Its highest branches will never touch the lowest clouds, but it continues to grow toward heaven.

The hard and salutary lesson of night should not be misinterpreted or shortened. For men, for poets, for saints, the testimonial of their "night" gives proof of a profound and indispensable experience. Nocturnal knowledge, as it is given expression to by Nerval, Baudelaire, Rimbaud, is at the very source of the greatest nineteenth century poetry. In these poets the human spirit had undergone "the terrible tenebrific purification" about which that saint of night has spoken, Saint John of the Cross, and thus had prepared the advent of the more luminous, more joyous poetic spirit of today. Claudel's work bears the double testimonial, first of night and then of that which is truly much more than a testimonial, because it is a conquest of day, of light, of joy. His work again resembles the tree which needs, in order to live, a double experience: the night's recollection and the morning's sun. His work is therefore the conquest of a domain very rarely penetrated by poets.

What opened up to Claudel his access to this domain? First, his robust nature of a simple man who is familiar with the fields of his village and who loves the farming of his fields. In a letter to Jacques Rivière he wrote: "Je suis un pauvre bonhomme tout plein du tracas des affaires et de la vie de famille." It is perhaps due to this side of his nature, that of a "pauvre bonhomme," which permitted him to experience the great simplicity of joy. And then, his encounter at the age of eighteen with the poetry of Rimbaud was immediately followed by a second encounter, his

meeting with God. Claudel's conversion, or rather the
return to the Catholicism of his childhood, didn't mark
an end to his struggles or the beginning of a period of
peace. His poetry of Christian inspiration is turbulent.
"Dieu est l'hôte qui ne vous laissera point de repos," he
wrote. Finding God doesn't assure tranquillity. The conquest of oneself is more terrifying for a believer than for a
non-believer because despair at failure becomes more and
more profound as the end is more known and more loved.

The difference between Claudel and the poets we call
the poets of night springs from two needs apparent in both
works: a need of negation with Claudel, which is a positive
need with the other poets; and a positive need with Claudel,
which is the contrary with the poets of night. The first
need, of a negative principle for Claudel, is a desire to
disappear from his work. It appears in his wish to be hidden
by his work, his effort to give to his work the sole reality.

Faites que je sois entre les hommes comme une
personne sans visage

is one of Claudel's most moving thoughts and one which
stands out in opposition with the need of the night poets
to attract attention personally to themselves. As darkness
becomes more complete, so do these poets try more to
articulate themselves, to describe themselves, to look at
themselves. With light is born the desire to dissolve
oneself, to efface oneself, so that the light alone may
endure.

The second need, of a positive principle with Claudel,
is the necessity which urges him to write integrally, to say
everything at once, to sing in each verse the unity of his
poet's credo. Experience with the night poets is divided and

cut up into parts. They name separately their objects, their symbols, their sentiments. They exploit the refinement of grief. In Claudel we become aware of an incoercible need to say everything. His vocation of a poet is intense and necessary. He has called his work "une explosion intelligible." The impatience of his soul causes him to put everything into a single ode: the sun, the summer, the day, the harvest, the flowers sticky with honey. His poem is orchestrated as no other poem is. His lyricism is a form of delirium. "Que je sois anéanti dans mon mouvement," he says in one of his odes. He is, in a word, the man who sings and thereby fulfils some hidden principle, as the tree is that object which bears branches and leaves.

II

If Claudel is a poet by the predestined vocation of his heart and temperament, what has been the major influence operating on his nature, what has been his formation, what was his heritage? For poets are heirs. They are born with their natures, but they receive, from without, a heritage which favors and develops their natures. Very often the heritage of a poet is the work of another poet. The heritage of Mallarmé is *Les Fleurs du Mal,* as the heritage of Valéry is Mallarmé's verse. For Rimbaud the principle heritage was not literary; it was more mysterious and complex. We might easily call it the heritage of memory, if by that were understood the ageless overflowing memory of a race which, through some miracle or other, came to light in a single man. The heritage of Claudel is the entire world. The word which his name inevitably calls to mind is the word "cosmos." Because of his profession of diplomat, as vice-consul and ambassador, he has lived in every part of the world: Boston, China, Austria, Italy, Brazil, Denmark, Japan, Washington. This is the geographical form of the world's heritage. In literatures he inherited the greatest and most enriching: the Greek, Latin, and Biblical literatures. From the poets he chose as his favorites those whose vision is the most grandiose and cosmic: Dante, Aeschylus, Shakespeare. Claudel perhaps asked for only one gift as heritage, but it was the world's totality. In one of his odes he hails this heritage of everything which, rather than dazzling him, only serves to strengthen him in his poet's mission:

> Salut donc, ô monde nouveau à mes yeux, ô monde maintenant total.

Before everything, before the entire world which waits like some inert matter, Paul Claudel rediscovers the old primitive vocation of a poet, the vocation of resurrecting the world. Everything must relive in a single work. As in Ulysses' voyage, as in the tragedy of human destiny sung by Sophocles, we find ourselves in Claudel's poetry in the presence of the primitive consecration of the earth and in the midst of the total movement of human effort. First, the entire world is in it: horizons, oceans, cities, houses, the furniture of each house. Then we find man in it, living at the very heart of the unbelievable richness of the world. And finally we see man in his relation with the universe, we follow his desire to utilize the universe in order to attain the First Source and total comprehension. All great poetry is by definition primitive because poets have never ceased being amazed at the universe. They have never forgotten their first vocation, formulated anew in the nineteenth century by Baudelaire, which is to seize the "profound and dark unity of things" (*la profonde et téné-breuse unité*).

Poetry of antiquity in its lyricism, in its epics, and in its tragedies, exalted man much more than the universe of man. The universe and man have equal places in Claudel's work, because the universe exists for man, and man, thanks to the universe, can begin to understand the reason for his existence. Man in antiquity is more tragic because he is less aware of this meaning of the universe. The works of antiquity, however beautiful and moving they may be, remain testimonials before man, whereas a truly Christian work must be a testimonial before God. Claudel is less easily comparable to the Greek poets, obsessed as they were with man's fatality, than he is comparable to the anonymous artisans and laborious philosophers of the French Middle Ages. In Claudel and in the mediaeval artisan we can discover the same effacement of self, the same desire to throw into relief man's work because the work testifies to something outside of man—to the eternal spirit of man, perhaps. For a Christian, man is always man and at the same time something greater than man. He must therefore abase himself and in a certain sense disappear from before his divine heritage. The meaning of charity, when it becomes clear to man, is the supreme gift. The representation of the universe in mediaeval art is never solely representation. It is innocency, faith, love, evil, prayer. It is very often joy. Simultaneously the mediaeval artist reveals the intrinsic beauty of nature and its theological value, its metaphysical sense. In antiquity and in the French classical period there is little of this direct sentiment about nature and this jubilant exaltation before the exterior world. In the eighteenth and nineteenth centuries nature is sung of without any other reason save for its changing, variable, indifferent beauty. Either it is greater than man, surer than he, more beautiful—or it is hostile to him in its aloofness and scorn. The belief that man is destined for God exists in many modern books, but after the Middle Ages we have found only in Claudel's work and in the work of a single other poet the belief, elaborated as an artistic theme, that the universe has for its end the One—that is, God.

The principal law for Claudel's poetic inspiration, as it was for all mediaeval arts, is the law of analogy. In his *Art Poétique*, Claudel writes: "Je comprends que chaque chose ne subsiste pas sur elle seule, mais dans un rapport infini avec toutes les autres." It is perhaps true that only Christian poets, when they are Christian in the total dogmatic sense of the word, can explicitly obey this law of analogy. In logical sequence, their works must rest upon analogy because their faith makes it necessary. God, creator of all things, calls them back to himself at the end. He leaves them with us for a time and thereby reveals himself, although imperfectly, to us. Joy for the Christian poet is the discovery of God everywhere. "O poète," Claudel has one of his characters say, "toutes choses par toi nous deviennent explicables."

This poetry of the universe, which is a poetry of Christian faith, because everything named is attached to a metaphysical principle, is eminently in Claudel's work, and to a degree almost as powerful and continuous, in the work of the English poet who was a Jesuit priest, Gerard Manley Hopkins. Claudel and Hopkins maintain the principle of analogy more constantly than other Christian poets such as Crashaw, Eliot, Péguy. Their song is more robust. It attacks the classical rules of versification, the laws of syntax and vocabulary—that is, all the lesser laws, as the Gothic cathedral scorned the classical laws of architecture. Faith gives to some men a boldness which is very capable of irritating other men. Poetry is the universe for Claudel and Hopkins, and it is also a closed house because it contains everything. There are lines in Claudel's ode, *La Maison Fermée*, which state the principle of analogy and make of it a kind of indestructible metaphysics:

O mon Dieu, qui avez fait toutes choses donnables, donnez-moi un désir à la mesure de votre miséricorde!

Afin qu'à mon tour à ceux-là qui peuvent le recevoir je donne en moi cela qui à moi-même est donné. . . .

O certitude et immensité de mon domaine! ô cher univers entre mes mains connaissantes! . . .

O Dieu, rien n'existe que par une image de votre perfection!

III

We named Claudel "the poet" who comes after certain artists in France, poets in their own right but not possessing the same total vigor and the same primitivism of the poetic talent. Then, we defined his heritage as being that of the entire world. It may be possible at this point to discover Claudel's secret and the key to his extensive work. For poets have secrets. The writing of each one is formed around a secret which is the *raison d'être* of the writing. It is the force which invokes the poetry, which demands the poetry, which belabors the mind of the poet, and which secretly invades all the verses and stanzas. Mallarmé's secret was the azure—the vast and unsounded purity of which each poem was an imperfection. Rimbaud's secret was intoxication, the state of the visionary, the physical and psychic state in which the poet could fix his attention upon his memory. Claudel's secret is something quite different. It is not like the azure of Mallarmé, which was an absence of images on which all the poetic images formed. It is not like Rimbaud's intoxication, which was the first dizziness of the adolescent facing all the universe and all that is not yet created. Claudel's secret is a problem in metaphysics. The essential word and key to his literary work is "knowledge."

In the passage of Claudel just quoted, there is a line whose meaning should be analyzed:

O cher univers entre mes mains connaissantes.

It is important to define as accurately as possible the meaning which Claudel ascribes to the verb "connaître" (know) and the substantive "connaissance" (knowledge). He points out first the negative formation of the verb "naître" (to be born: ne-être). When we are born, we leave God. Our birth is our separation from God. In other words, when we are born, we are not what is because God alone is. But we are never born alone because we are born with the universe, into the universe, in relationship with all the elements of the universe. Knowledge (co-naissance) is therefore birth (naissance) with all things created by God. A poet like Claudel knows the things of the earth more intimately than most men, because he feels and longs for a birth with the first primitive universe, namely Paradise. Paradise was the first creation and man was born first with it. Claudel's secret seems to be his desire to be born with the first paradisaic universe and to lead the world back into its initial rôle of happiness and perfection. "The knowing hands" of the poet attempt this prodigious effort. As the hands of the priest placed over the bread transform it into a divine substance, so do the hands of the poet over the common matter of the universe transform it into the primitive and perfect matter of the first creation. These are two miracles: the priest's miracle which is true, and the poet's miracle which is false or symbolic because it is the miracle of art.

The history of human thought and the history of art could be written in terms of the divers explanations of this word "knowledge." One might begin in antiquity with the celebrated precept of Socrates, "Know thyself," and then study its Thomistic explanation in the Middle Ages. One might isolate a sentence of Rimbaud which appears in his *Lettre du Voyant:* "La première étude de l'homme qui veut être poète est sa propre connaissance entière," and then study its application in Claudel's work. We no longer hesitate to say that philosophical knowledge, so disastrously attacked by modern thinking, is going to survive thanks to what we might call poetic knowledge. Poets and critics of poetry have revindicated the rights of metaphysics. At all periods in history the bonds between philosophy and poetry have appeared close, but mysterious and difficult to define. This dilemma is vigorously rejected by Claudel, who appears as the great lover of the problem of metaphysics, as the conqueror of the problem. The unity of his entire work is the reprisal, in each part of the work, of the major themes of metaphysics. Consider the following line from one of his odes:

pas un souffle de ma vie que je ne prenne à votre éternité

in order to see with what insolence Claudel poses and resolves the immense problems of the relationship between man and God, and between time and eternity.

It is true that poets are more insolent and more bold than philosophers, but it is because they are freer. They steal the verbs of philosophers and give them revolutionary meanings. "To know" (connaître) becomes for the poets a synonym of the verb "to be" (être: "to be" in accordance with man's principle and not in accordance with God's). And then "to be" (être) becomes a synonym of the verb "to create" (créer: "to create" in accordance with man's principle and not in accordance with God's). Simply because poets are, do they know. The poetry of Claudel is simply that, and the concept of liberty could not be defined in more vertiginous terms.

Men do not create as God creates, that is evident. In order to create their work, they need everything that has already been created. But God also, curiously, in order to create, needs His own creation. He needed a woman for His Incarnation. God, at one moment in time, needed Mary's consent. And today, still, in order to create a new soul, God needs the consent of a man and a woman.

The birth of man with the universe perpetuates the drama of knowledge which is universal, uninterrupted, unending. At the beginning of our study we stated this thought, that man is a prisoner because he is a part of the creation. Man cannot be elsewhere save in the creation, but it is there he finds God because he is born with the created things of God.

Vous êtes ici et je ne puis être autre part qu'avec vous.

The liberty of this captive is real, however. It is with his poet's voice that he can create "eternal things." In this same ode we have just quoted, the poet sees the rose perish, but its name does not perish from his mind:

son nom dans l'esprit qui est mon esprit ne périt plus.

The drama of knowledge does not cease being a drama as long as it remains in the universe. It is solely in the poetic work, in that strange celebration of words, that it is resolved and approaches another state which we shall call the joy of knowledge.

IV

After the secret of poets, comes the symbol of the secret. After Mallarmé's azure, after Rimbaud's intoxication, after Claudel's knowledge, comes the achievement in art, the poetic exploitation. Azure, intoxication, knowledge, are not susceptible of immediate translation: they have to be converted into another more symbolic language. Mallarmé's azure became a series of concrete symbols: a faun, a tomb, a swan. Rimbaud's intoxication was symbolized by hell, the domain where the soul becomes monstrous. And finally, Claudel's knowledge is translated by joy, by the religious sentiment of joy. It is not necessary to share Claudel's faith in order to feel its expression in his work. Faith is experience for Claudel, as evil was for Baudelaire, as passion was for Racine, as religious suffering was for Pascal. A great art does not require us to undergo the same experience from which it has arisen; its only requirement is that we heed the form given to that experience.

Claudel, in one of his letters to Jacques Rivière, has a sentence which has guided us in this study. "Tout artiste vient au monde pour dire une seule chose." With this in mind, we have been searching for the unique revelation in Claudel's poetry. We believed first to have discovered it in his sanctification of the world, but now we believe to have found it more truly in his sanctification of joy. The world is never ready for joy; it is always surprised by the apparition of joy. And especially our world, our poor world with its cumbersome heritage of the nineteenth century which had taught it to forget God. Our world, tired of warfare and haunted by the perspective of still more complicated wars, has become the setting for Claudel's joy. It is a joy of superabundance and excess which will live longer than the wretched and sad history of our age. The place which Claudel occupies, his midway place, between the men who give themselves to the world and the saints who give themselves to God, will end perhaps in becoming the most radiant place in our world for the ages to come. The place of poets grows with time and ends by throwing into obscurity the lesser values of a period. This prophetic tone is pardonable on the basis that in Claudel's work we encounter not only the first essential lesson of the poet, which is the losing of oneself in the thing loved, but in addition we learn a second lesson, through the sanctification of joy, which is the losing of the thing loved in oneself.

The long years in Claudel's life spent far from France recall Dante's exile. Voluntary exile for both poets permitted them to know a more intense love for the thing left. The accent of joy expressed at the end of the *Divine Comedy* and in certain pages of Claudel is an exclusive kind of passion felt by the exile who has passed through suffering. This quality of joy, which is exclusive and powerful, is the cause of the irritation which Claudel's work excites very often. But truth also is exclusive. The joy we refer to is harsh and solitary. In a dance of Miss Martha Graham, our most significant artist in the American theatre today, we can also see a representation of impersonal and exclusive joy. The dance is called *El Penitente*, at the end of which, after scenes of struggle and agony, the three characters: the penitent, the Virgin, and Christ remove their actors' garments, their masks, and their very sentiments in order to dance joy. The three come forward, dressed in white trousers or in a white dress, to dance alone or together because joy came upon them and arrested the drama. In Martha Graham's dance, as in many passages of Claudel, the virtue of joy follows the truth of drama. They contain a trace of flamboyant Catholicism, the Catholicism of great ceremony, and a trace of the total uncontrolled joy which Protestantism has never understood.

Il n'est à ce discours parole ou son, pause ou sens,
Rien qu'un cri, la modulation de la Joie, la Joie même qui s'élève et qui descend,
O Dieu, j'entends mon âme folle en moi qui pleure et qui chante!

But the century is opposed to joy. What we know today above all is the caricature of joy. Nothing is more bitter than the comic trait of *The New Yorker*, of the Broadway musical review, of the Hollywood productions. We are completely servile in the domain of the comic. We seem to laugh exclusively at the weak or perverse sides of human nature.

The comic is too near the tragic. It is the domain of Molière and Proust; it is not Claudel's domain. The comic is an integral part of Dante's *Inferno*; it does not exist in his *Paradiso*. Joy is vastly different from comedy. It is far away from comedy, detached, living apart in a sphere closed to weakness, irony, bitterness. We are able to penetrate it only after we exceed ourselves and after our birth with all the inferior sentiments.

Claudel gives us the portrait of a man who finds in his joy a better knowledge of himself. Each work of his is an explosion in which the poet seems bent upon overturning an entire system. He repudiates the most austere sentiments and denounces the most stable beliefs. But he pursues this work of demolition in order to rebuild afterwards, to reassemble, to reintegrate. And the new system, which is the old system reconstructed, reappears on a surer foundation. Claudel is both demolisher and builder. He is the poet of energy. Gerard Manley Hopkins is of the same race of poets. We are more accustomed to the poets whose work is better explained by the term "willfulness." The poetry of Mallarmé and T. S. Eliot, for example, grows laboriously and patiently by this force we call "willfulness" whereas the force which animates the poetry of Claudel and Father Hopkins is quite different. In the realm of painting, the canvases of Picasso can give the same effect as the poetry of Claudel. Picasso's energy, also, upsets the world and what remains on the finished picture is a delirious kind of joy, so intense that it ends by becoming the artist's personality.

Joy is Claudel's goal. It breaks out everywhere without revealing exactly its source or its manner. Joy in Claudel's work becomes the fact one accepts without explanation. We have seen how easy it is to understand in Claudel's conception the metaphysics of knowledge, and in it we have perhaps come upon a formula of art which teaches us that in the creative thoughts of a man of energy and valor, a total metaphysics of knowledge inevitably engenders joy.

THE POET AND THE MYSTIC

The channel of freedom

FREEDOM IS BORN only from faith. When man attains faith in some being or in some body of doctrine, he envisages it as a reservoir, encompassed by banks, but so vast that his needs and desires would never necessitate the reaching of the banks. It is therefore erroneous to talk of limitations or fetters of any absolute belief; they are not that to a believer, but rather his source of liberty. He knows there is no other alternative, no other truth. His freedom comes from this knowledge of the inadequacy and the emptiness of anything beyond the limits of his reservoir. His life is spent in the absorption of a part of what he has made his own. In the hierarchy of faiths, that of the love of one individual for another is one of the most common and one whose image is frequently used to designate symbolically other faiths. The psychological experience of love is similar to that of all faiths. During the profoundest moments of love, the rest of the world disappears as though it ceased to exist, and the lovers remain bathed in waters from which they long never to emerge.

Paradoxically the mystic, as he progresses in his spiritual experience, discovers more and more liberty in his ever-narrowing sphere. The unitive way is that of detachment for concentration. During the period of so-called freedom, the mystic's activity is one of conquest; and, as the end of this conquest is unattainable during his life time, there can be no relaxation of effort. It is in this effort and conquest

130

taking place during a beloved freedom that the activity of the poet first resembles that of the mystic. The poet, when functioning as such, both wills and desires an attitude and a spiritual insight which set him off from his fellow men and isolate him from the familiar universe. It is needless to point out that the world knows but few true mystics and true poets, and that their vocations are fully justified only during brief minutes. To know ecstasy and to write poetry, there is required nothing less than an entire life of a special experience, a willed abnegation and a long-enduring conquest.

If it is true that the poet works in freedom, his art itself is liberty. The result of his unfettered delectation is the delectation, not a mere symbol but the reality. The poet is not a poet until he has composed and achieved. The object wrought by the artist is the liberty toward which he has been striving, the point outside time which both sums up and subsumes time. In contemplation of it, the artist reviews struggles, aesthetics, faiths which have been channelled during a foreknowledge of liberty toward the realization of liberty, toward the veritable creation of liberty.

Prayer is the poem of the mystic, the tangible achievement of his liberty, which admits him to more lucid understanding of the world he has renounced and to a foreknowledge of the supernatural. Neither the poet nor the mystic teaches. Both bear testimonials to an explanation, but their work is no commentary or exegesis. The only lesson a poet and a mystic can give, and it is hardly a lesson at all, is precisely the example of the supreme liberty they have attained through the prefigurement of liberty.

It is never the mystery of the poem which should startle or confound the reader. The verses themselves are no mask or labyrinth. The seat of all obscurity is in the poet. His life and his thoughts are the only approximate key possible. And how difficult they are of any approach! The severing of bonds, the dissolution of entanglements, and the other various steps he has made toward the conception of freedom have released him and have introduced him to a new image of the universe. The reader most prone to see in the poetic work obscurantism and irrationality is still caught in the manifold bonds which habitually enslave him and from which the poet has extricated himself. The poet's adversary is the non-free man, and he is in most cases the same one who attacks most vehemently the mystic. He will be prevented from becoming the poet's partisan as long as he succeeds in convincing himself that there are particles of truth everywhere or that truth is invented and distributed by man or that there is no poetry and mysticism in insanity!

Madness, become sanity and the way of life in freedom, could therefore be a simplified definition of a state or experience of those who deliberately set themselves off from the world and thus are better able to understand it. Liberty consummated in ecstasy or poetic creation seems to be a kind of response, a reward vouchsafed to ardor and labor. But this response is no effusion of sentiment; this liberty is no spontaneous bubbling-over of emotion. It is a dedication of the will, a conscious election, an imposition fastened, in most cases, on a restive nature. Entrance upon the state of liberty is no escape from suffering and no self-indulgence. There will be there the same oscillations of pleasure and pain, only accentuated and heightened. Saint Theresa's words, "Let me suffer and die," are a poignant testimonial to the mystic's new comprehension of and desire for suffering. Pain for both mystic and poet is the measurer of strength and the guardian of cherished liberty.

The will to obedience

Of the three-fold monastic vow: poverty, chastity, obedience, the last named has a parallel participation in the poet's credo. The liberty so necessary for poetic and saintly vigor, is arrived at through no other means than that of the will's impoverishment. When it is said that no genius can afford to spend wastefully his energies, it is meant his will should be depleted and subjugated. He must will to obey and thus separate himself from everything but the reality of his vocation in much the same way as the saint must will to detach himself from everything but the reality of the Godhead. This is what I think can rightfully be called the poverty of the will. It is a violent form of mortification and therefore only a means to an end. The line of Thomas-à-Kempis, "If we were perfectly dead to ourselves," may be interpreted in this light. When the saint and the poet are not dead to themselves, when their wills are not dedicated and submitted, they are susceptible to a grave danger, the danger of an artist's lie and a mystic's hypocrisy. When Jacopone da Todi sings of poverty, he sings also of the poverty of the will. To wish for nothing is to possess everything in the spirit of liberty:

> Povertate è nulla avere
> e nulla cosa poi volere.

This regimen of life for the mystic involves the turning away from all impurity; for the poet it involves the effacement of the ordinary vision of the universe. Symbols and meanings, visions and harmonies are the new universe imposed upon the former one. What he sees is a transposition, what he hears is an orchestration. The muse is an unveiler of analogies.

What is commonly referred to as the illuminated life is the life in which mystics and artists alike share in varying degrees. The light is a captured apprehension of the oneness in the world, of the imperishable beauty against which they had unwittingly striven heretofore. No spirit whose will is still active and who hasn't plunged into the reservoir of freedom, thereby washing himself of vainglory and pretence, can hope to see the infinite simplicity promised the pure in heart. The very symbol of light, which is the recurrent explanation of mysticism and of which Dante makes the most exalted use in his *Paradiso*, indicates the degree of abeyance the mind must be maintained in for the flood of purity. No matter how much struggle or effort precedes the relinquishment of the will's power, the advent of light seems to require passivity. It comes after abdication and brings in its wake the new experience for the human spirit which we might call an added significance of the universe or, in some extreme cases, a totally remade significance. This state of receptivity, this heroism of obedience, is the true miracle residing in the poet and the mystic. The poem is at best but an imperfect replica of vision, understanding, and analogy. The mystic, whose experience is more profound than that of the poet, acknowledges his incapacity to translate it. Ineffability is his state. Afterwards, if he writes, it will perhaps be a hymn of praise, not a recapture of his joy. But the poet whose joy is less, may lead us nearer his.

The real activity which the will renounces is the expenditure of energy useless to the ultimate end of existence. The mediaevals who taught that the principle of all art is the ultimate end ("cum in operabilibus principium et causa omnium sit ultimis finis"—Dante, *De Monarchia*), were restating a thought of Aristotle. The will obedient has not renounced the world itself, but the "remora" of the world. The light of illumination which follows willed subservience is a ravishment of eternity, a union with invulnerability. This is indeed the true mark of the mystic. Is it not a similar mark of the poet, even of the poet hostile to religious conviction? Even as there are two ways for the mystic to apprehend God, namely, that of transcendence and that of immanence, so there seem to be two ways for the poet to liberate himself: the will bound to the last end or the will bound to symbols of the universe, a union which by its very infinity is a protection against the world's remora and an unrecognized secondary source to invulnerability.

The artist must know as well as the mystic the solitude of recollection at the end of which there takes place in his nature an invasion. The world will or the Divine Will, no matter how it be defined, is the invader and conqueror. The man in both the poet and mystic, after he has passed through the dull and arid period of quiet despair in loneliness, feels the strange encounter with the will greater than his, the meeting he has willed in order to renounce will. This encounter must be a happiness for the mystic and a recognition for the poet, a kind of merited patrimony. With happiness and recognition, there takes place a self-merging which is in the figurative sense the fertilization of aridity. For the mystic it is the inception of the illuminated life; for the poet it is the creation of his world of symbols, the poetic reality behind reality, the indefinable vastness which like night itself embraces all suffering and ecstasy, all oblivion and knowledge.

Communication and ineffability

In the *Imitation* we read, "No man securely governs but he who would willingly live in subjection." It is not difficult to consider the new poetic and mystical liberty discussed in the preceding remarks as a government based upon a belief in the insecurity of this life. Man not created for leadership but to undergo domination; man not the director of his own projects but the testifier to a human awareness of divine ordination. The mystic is a veritable well of receptivity and the poet a labyrinth of symbols. This is the deep and mysterious character of the man serving humanity as a communication between two realities. "For ye have not received the spirit of bondage again to fear; but ye have received the Spirit of adoption," writes Saint Paul in his Epistle to the Romans. Bondage to fear would be no liberty; but the spirit of adoption, of filial relationship and recognition, releases the images of communication on the one side and seals up the fountains of speech on the other.

Whereas the poet dwells and moves in a multiplicity of consciousness, in a rhythm of progagation, the mystic rises in the oneness of love, in the quiet of self-donation. For the first, physical words conceal a life of suggestion and dilatation; they reflect adumbrations and trace contours; they achieve a finiteness of the hated ego; they speak in measured tones of an unmeasured universe. For the second, quiet and recollection increase in a certitude more absolute than any other. Activity becomes the embrace of certitude, the total estrangement from multiplicity and the union with the One.

The poet travels toward a broadening and crowded horizon, while the saint turns inward to a contracted sphere of the reinvigorated self. Visions and new states of consciousness for Rimbaud the "voyant"; for him, derangement and secular memory. But for Dionysius the Areopagite, the stillness and light of Divine Darkness. For the poet, experience terminates in expression; for the mystic, experience commences with silence.

Despite the one purpose of contemplation common to all mystics, mystical literature reveals a great diversity of images. This very diversity testifies to the inadequacy of the written word. The life of the contemplative is essentially an unseen life. In terms of the world, his knowledge is unknowable and his music ghostly. In the work of poets whose experience comes closest to the mystical experience, the impressions transcribed often have the quality of being infused, of being dictated rhythms and images. These are the poets whose intuition would seem to be the revelation of the sum, whose verses seem fragments of a life-giving completedness. If poetry is to be different from prose, it must be charged with more meaning and more music. Neither meaning nor music is arrived at ultimately by explanations and exposition. The carefully constructed prose dissertations of the great philosophers contradict one another and vie in sophistry and logic. In the realm of perception they may be defeated by a fragment of a verse or a stanza.

The ineffability of rapture seems to be nothing more or less than the ineffability of certitude, the unspeakableness of absolute liberty. The ravishment of Saint Paul to the third heaven and the ecstasies of Pascal are the attainment to Pure Spirit; even more than attainment, they are the welding of human spirit into Divine Spirit. Thus the end of orison is achieved.

If orison were conceived of as a long road ending in a vast field where the pilgrim rests inebriated by a divine effulgence, the very road with its pitfalls and wonders, its daylight and darkness, its easy stages and difficult ones, might be the same travelled over by the artist who reproduces in his art the overtones and undertones of pitfalls and wonders and who never attains the moment about which nothing can be recorded. The words of poets witness to an incomplete and unfulfilled experience. A pitfall provokes composition about joy. Happiness during its stage rarely if every inspires the pen.

The adolescent sensibility of a poet matured by years, his perceptions and atttiudes, his one-way road, and his sorrows which the world can apprehend but not diminish are far less mysterious than the intervals during which he composes. These moments are the temptation to sadness, the disengaging of his self and the perishing of his silence. They are the poet's Dark Night of the Soul during which the mystic would feel aridity and emotional lassitude. To live them the poet must annihilate himself and become the worker in his own laboratory of symbols. The mystic's goal is precisely annihilation of self during which he experiences an unwritten and silenced felicity.

Rimbaud, the mystical poet

More clearly than other modern poets, those born from the indecisive and tragic nineteenth century, Rimbaud chiseled in his verses and decisive prose a vigor emanating from tenderness, a life communicated by rhythm and images. Rimbaud the poet savored sombre things, appropriated despair and temptation common to all men, and sought to live them and surpass them in cynicism, blasphemy, immorality. But his very impetuosity has a virginal mildness; his mockery is tearful and nostalgic.

This poet who wrote between the ages of sixteen and twenty, having experienced the crises of maturity, illustrates admirably the line of Saint Paul, "But God is faithful, who will not suffer you to be tempted above that ye are able." Rimbaud rose to the stature of a great poet by struggling with Herculean tasks, by feeling within himself a work surging and forming. When he calls the poet the "sombre savant d'orgueil" he gives evidence of a presentiment of the poetic sign, the mystic's knowledge of solitude. The wound which seemed to fill his entire being he called "une blessure éternelle"; it was the wound common to all, which marked Rimbaud with the past and future.

The insanity of visionaries inhabits this adolescent poet who advocates total derangement of the senses in order to become his breed of visionary. Saint Martin's phrase, "I heard flowers that sounded, and saw notes that shone," resembles the modern poetic credo. Readings, vagabond flights, realization of natural youthful impulses, dreams of the virgin knight, gestures of first loves are Rimbaud's adventure and his frantic search. One treasure and one dream after another are examined and discarded; the search continues relentlessly and it is a search comparable to that of a mystic who, blinded, would see in darkness. It is the search of a poet who, wounded, forces himself on to a liberty he subconsciously knows exists and which is at hand:

"In that thou hast sought me, thou hast already found me."

Rimbaud's much discussed flight from literature and his abstinence from the written word are merely the result of the weighted sadness most artists have felt upon realization of art's innate and unsatisfactory approximations. Through the deepening of the same delicacy which had made an artist of Rimbaud, he abandoned a poet's vocation. The clarity of transposition increased to such a degree that he ended by seeing that which is impossible of transcription. We can only faintly imagine the whirlwind of light that struck him. One of the exquisite prose poems bears the title, *Aube*. At the beginning the child fell in the depths of the woods. Rimbaud's embrace of light led to his death by it.

Before this mystic death, the poet's work, meagre in its number of pages, gives some indication of the fecundity of his spirit and his vision of the universe's immensity. What men have too frequently called the work of genius is here before us: a meeting place of eternity and a human soul, the miraculously reinvented measures of man's voice. The genius is both the master of silence and its slave. The poet exists not only in the words to which he signs his name, but he is also in the whiteness which remains on the page. His honesty is his intactness, and Rimbaud gloriously lived intact.

Throughout *Une Saison en Enfer* Rimbaud struggles with the angel to extract his blessing. In successive touches he relives the past and prophesies the future. A gamut of full tones and half tones, marches, defeats, victories, all resound and reverberate, all harmonize in a completed whole. One sentence above all stands denuded in its severity: "Je veux la liberté dans le salut." It is a line which overflows with meaning and which by its very conciseness testifies to the vastness of unknown love. Rimbaud the imprisoned poet wills liberty in salvation! How impossible it is to imagine the birth of such a desire, if Rimbaud hadn't seen the world's bitter dawns or if the tempest hadn't blest his maritime sleeplessness.

The thought of the prophet Jeremiah is strangely applicable to all poets: "And the Lord said unto me, Behold, I have put my words in thy mouth." The poet's charity is a bewitched one in the eyes of the world. Rimbaud bestowed a sorcerer's spell. Brief notations of the inexpressible hardly constitute a testament to be read and assimilated by the populace. By fixing in words a fugitive and wounded sensibility, he endowed it with a freedom unknown to himself. He discovered in a single being the multiple lives that were owing to it. In this activity he was the poet. His subsequent evasion was the explanation of his poetry.

Jacopone da Todi, the poetic mystic

The true poet, when a mystic, is the seeker; the true mystic, when a poet, is the recorder. The function of the poet is that of doing; the function of the mystic is that of being. As a poet, Jacopone da Todi is in nowise comparable to Rimbaud. The visions of Rimbaud were finite and still possess today a marvelous communicability. But the madness of Fra Jacopone, like his poem on the Last Judgment, announces such an otherworldliness, such a lack of measure ("summa smesuranza"), that the beauty he attempts to put in verse, fades until it becomes a work of no color. This absence of color in the beauty he contemplates is unquestionably a greater spiritual achievement than a poetic image to be recorded:

Tutto lo suo sentire
en ben sì va notando,
belleza contemplando
la qual non ha colore.

Rimbaud's poetry was a mortification leading to health. The tertiary brother of Saint Francis, when he wrote, was already breathing a salubrious air other than that of the Umbrian hills.

Jacopone consummates his death in singing. Love by which he is wounded is a delight and a death. He can live only without a heart. Jacopone played a definite part in the Franciscan movement of the thirteenth century which accentuated the humanity of Christ and gave a central position to the Cross. He sings of Christ as the Divine Flower. The purity and suavity of this Flower have a reflected counterpart in the poet himself. The humiliation of the Flower and its effulgent resurrection, the Flower pointing out its sweet-smelling flowers to the doubting disciple, all have a poetic validity. Repetition and canticle simplicity, dithyrambic insistence and rhythmical monotony force the tone of art's subservience to inspiration. In a poet who is more exclusively a poet than Jacopone da Todi, this subservience is never consciously expressed or apparent. The song of the one wounded by love and dying by it is vastly different in its hammered clarity from the song of the one who yearns for love's wounds, not having experienced them.

The miracle of a poetic work coming from a mystical experience is its unity of theme and its constancy of images. Love makes Jacopone sing. The state of inebriation to which this love has reduced him is inevitably transcribed by the split or perforated heart, the furnace of fire, the blindness which comes from Divine Light. In his experience he is the receiver and in his poetry he is the transmitter of what he received. But because this transmission is usually couched in terms of physical imagery is no reason for believing that it is an accurate transcription of experience, a scientific analysis of psychical transport. For here Jacopone is the poet and the gates are always closed to what lies beyond the poetic word. All poetry is ultimately a paradox. The mystical paradox of Jacopone's poetry may be summed up in this way: in living he dies; in dying he lives. This in itself is a profoundly poetic message. But only Jacopone held the key to its source.

> Amore, amor, dove m'hai tu menato?
> Amore, amor, fuor de me m'hai tirato,
> Amore, amor, non so dove sia andato,
> chè sono entrato—en fornace d'amore.

The verses of Jacopone do not make up a literature of edification. When his verses are poetry, they are usually based upon antithesis and paradox which both approximate and veil the spiritual experience. They are the verses which indicate the new existence of the man who becomes conqueror as soon as he desires to fight. How else could the madness of Jacopone, the mystic's apanage in terms of the world, be described? The love he desires makes him die of love ("Amor, cui tanto bramo, famme morir d'amore"); by keeping silent, he speaks ("tacendo parlo"); he hunts and is hunted ("caccio e so' cacciato"). When his verses are not poetry, they become a cry. Art is absconded for passion. Many stanzas and pages of this type of verse writing encircle the gems of his poetry.

The striking *Ballata Del Paradiso*, quite probably composed by Jacopone da Todi, paints the picture of a large wheel of saints and prophets and virgins who, made youthful, dance and sing before Christ in Paradise. It is a work of harmony and freshness and springtime, a work which taken with the poems written about Saint Francis of Assisi, illustrates the vision of the mystical poet and the prophet-like seriousness of his judgment of the world. The vision of a more spiritual Christendom and a reformed world castigates the age in which it took place. It is the Franciscan vision of the thirteenth century, reflected in the writings of Rutebeuf in France, in the *Divina Commedia,* and somewhat later in the fourteenth century in the English mystical poem, *Piers Plowman.* Even for the contemplative mystic, if he turns to art, devotion may lead to good works. Jacopone's verses rebound from God's gift of the will to love and from poverty's breast sheltering deity.

Wilderness and Eden

How is the poet the philosopher? The beauty he creates, in creating himself, is not truth but it is limited by and in subservience to truth. The pleasure we experience in reading a page of noble poetry is a pleasure of moral man conscious or quasi-conscious of his last end. Poetry is not truth. Poetry is not life. It is consciousness of both. The poet doesn't seek truth as the philosopher or the scientist; but he is governed by truth in his fusion of moral elements and aesthetic elements. When truth is making its demands upon the artisan, that is, during the period when he is constructing his cathedral or composing his poem, he is not seeking truth but working in its service. The intelligence which a Dante brings to the execution of his work is in reality wisdom akin to the gift of the Holy Spirit because it is wisdom which does not stop with knowledge but with love.

The poet has a work to perform. His wilderness verse may be humanity-impregnated verse. The mystic has a union to consummate: God loved was the purpose of Eden. This garden site of unreasonableness is the supreme décor for passion. The poet dwells on a drier land and acts when he chastens passion.

Man is the imitative animal. But imitation is a continuance and no futile impoverishment. Maritain writes in *Art et Scolastique,* "La création artistique ne copie pas celle de Dieu, elle la continue." If the artist tends toward the beauties of the world and by imitating them continues the act of creation, the mystic tends toward the Beauty above beauties, the eternally fixed Beauty of which all lesser beauties are the imitation. The existence of this supernal Beauty is the source of artistic integrity, proportion and clarity. These three are the conditions for beauty according to Saint Thomas Aquinas. They form, so to speak, tyrannical prerequisites for beauty and are apprehended by the ratiocinative powers of the artist. Here the poet is philosopher and subscribes to the classical doctrine of imitation of the universal.

In the artist's search to express beauty by creating it, it must be remembered that he doesn't create from a void, that is, he doesn't take something from nothing, and that the beauty he succeeds in expressing in a sonnet or in a painting is beauty expressed in himself. Maritain deftly defines this imitation in art by the term, "spiritual resemblance." It is Emerson's intuition of eternal beauty. The mystic's quest is a more direct one, less intuitive, and is realized not in resemblance to Absolute Beauty but in participation within Absolute Beauty.

The poet and the mystic, both sentient beings and joined

by their use of what can be called nothing less than centrifugal powers, are however separated by the degree of their experience. Wilderness and Eden: two lands created from the same void by the same mystery. Sterility and fertility: two testimonials to the same love! The poet utilizes this mysterious love; the mystic knows it.

THE MODERN POET

THE AUTHENTICITY OF an artist is in his completeness. No fragmentary art, no interrupted speech will assure communication. It is, of course, communication which is the artist's motive for work and his goal, whether it be in the species of communication in beauty, in rhythm, or in intellection. Completeness does not equate size, nor does it equate completion. We are not going to judge a work of art by the number of pages or by the number of poems or even by the state of its structural completion. More profound and more essential than all such measurements, completeness is that unity of tone which a single artist, working within the limitations of his own spirit, can give to the material he has elected: stone, words, pigment, sound. In these his voice will take on its own modulation, familiar to all those who are familiar with the medium, and new to all those who are attentive to the complexities of expression and life.

Whether it be a vast world or a small one, the artist's expression must be a world. The wholeness of Dante's art in his *Divine Comedy* and the wholeness of Gérard de Nerval's in his few sonnets, testify to this principle. Being is not broken up into parts by either poet; yet one has formed a tremendous world of philosophy and theology, of history and mythology; and the other, a minute world of absolute moments of lucidity which pierce and congeal dream, fancy, insanity. Dante has the eye which magnifies and dramatizes the life of facts. Nerval has the heart which

diminishes and fecundates the death of dreams. But mar-
velously in the work of both, everything exists, and everything is transformed and reconstructed according to the laws
of man's creation.

Completeness in art, which is its authentic nature, may
be conceived of as being a series of concentric circles of light,
one on the other, each of a different and distinctive color,
and the sum of them all forming the new color which is the
color of the work itself. The beauty of a thing created by
man seems to come from the mingling of the three major
circles: the moral, the metaphysical, and the spiritual or the
mystical. This image of concentric circles is a recast of the
mediaeval doctrine concerning the three-fold symbolistic
interpretation of art. Dante discusses this in his letter to
Can Grande. He refers to the moral meaning as the trope
and to the spiritual meaning as the anagoge. Allegory he
treats as being the interpretation of art suggested by some
event in the life of Christ. For our own ends, the allegorical
circle might be renamed the metaphysical one and in nowise prevent the Christian from seeing in the art of any
age or any philosophy a relation to the life of the Incarnate
Christ.

A work of art, therefore, which measures up to the standard of completeness, will contain in itself divers elements of
a moral, metaphysical and religious nature, the totality of
which will represent its creator's view of life. In certain
cases (and this will be evident in much contemporary art)
one of these spheres almost disappears. But here, the
absence itself has great weight and significance. The purely
aesthetic does exist in literature, as it does in every art, but
it is impossible to perceive it divorced from what is said
about the conduct of man or the belief of man. The aesthe-

tic, which is the formal element and which is addressed to the senses, will exist whether the writer be Christian or pagan, or whether he be primarily a philosopher or a poet. The interrelation between the form and the content of a work of art is comparable to a mystery of religion. This does not mean an abdication of reason or ingenuity. The work of art exists. (As, in another realm, faith exists.) But how the fulfillment of the laws of beauty came about within the province of man's thought has never yet, to our knowledge, been described. Somehow all that we can say about this matter is: art is, communication is, faith is. What we can perceive, however, is that their manifestations have varying degrees of power and profundity. Man is always man. And this is somewhat of a mystery. But man knows with marked precision when he is untrue to his state of being man. Art is always art. And we leave the mystery at that. But through the long process of time and through the persistent pleasure which art accords the senses and the mind of man, some element of its reality can be sounded and then recognized in a new work.

It is possible in a canto of the *Divine Comedy* or in a sonnet of Mallarmé to analyze a modulated thought, to apprehend in a metaphor a familiar emotion, to delight in an unfamiliar experience transcribed by a symbol. It is possible in a Bach fugue or a Mozart symphony to analyze the consonancy of successive sounds, to apprehend the proportions of a begun and completed tonal monument, to delight in the integrity of a controlled and audible light. Art demands of us this disciplined attentiveness in order that our intelligence take pleasure in its beauty. But behind the canto and the sonnet, which are but the sonority of a daily act and the color of a minute, there is a universe of symbols, a rich and profound décor abiding with the spirit of the artist. This spirit has lived before the art was created and continues to live after the art has been separated from its creator. There is behind the fugue and the symphony the music of the spheres which Pythagoras heard, the music which David heard in silent nights and which he did not transpose in his psalms.

Man makes the work of man. Before passing into form or matter, it takes its birth in the intelligence of man. Once separated from the artist, the work of art will be subjected to all the vicissitudes of a material object and will be loved and judged by the intelligence of man. The too absolute phrase, "invulnerability of art," may be applied simply to those works of art which, reflecting something of the spiritual reality common to all men, can be comprehended by successive centuries. It has not, strictly speaking, a terminal character, but has, rather, a measure of spirituality. Poetry is not the search for God, but the harmony of a moment when the search might have been undertaken. A poem testifies to an experience, but an arrested experience and one deformed by words. The poem exists by itself, truncated from the spiritual reality of the experience. Thus, the making of any work of art involves the danger of an immediate explanation. The permanent problem of man, in any race, in any age, is the understanding of his spiritual experience. His art, having its roots in this experience, translates it inadequately and lasts only in so far as it is fashioned upon some lines of beauty which are communicable and which give pleasure. Man's adventure is immutable; man's art is composed of varying and innumerable faces, incidents, and moments of his adventure.

The modern age, embracing a new faith in man and offering to the ills of humanity a man-invented cure, has relegated to an obscure place the true source of his enlightenment and joy. Potentially gifted artists have vitiated their work with a superabundance of human passion uncontrolled and unpurified by spirit. The art of Byron, Hugo, Wagner suffers from a wanton display of ego and sensuality, from purely human colors strident with overbalance and dissoluteness. From the poetic voices of the nineteenth century one is heard today above the others. This voice of Charles Baudelaire in centuries to come may be the representative voice of our period as Dante's is for us the representative voice of the fourteenth century. The very title of Baudelaire's work, *Les Fleurs du Mal,* witnesses to the age of which it is a product and to its subject jealously guarded over by both the good and the bad angels.

But art is not concerned primarily with morality. Here is poetry composed as flowers whose perfume poisons. Here is a poet who is a seat of frenzy and who has entered a universe apprehended as a multiplicity of signs. His spirit, whose quality was molded by a life of thoughts, moved in an adverse world. Without man's freedom of action, Baudelaire's poetry would be inexplicable. Yet as art it owes no servitude to chance.

Beauty is the fruit of patience and of hours free to die. Baudelaire's poems are brief representations of moments filled grievously by a sinister experience. Rimbaud's poems are also elliptical syntheses of moments crammed to the exploding point. The force of Baudelaire and the exasperation of Rimbaud cannot easily be attached to any other century than the nineteenth. Everything in their age had told them coldly and succinctly that they are alone and that their art will be the agony of their solitude and their misery. Baudelaire will call upon Satan for pity and Rimbaud will apostrophize Christ as the eternal thief of energies.

Baudelaire was the artist of the darkness which surrounded him, whereas Rimbaud was not only its artist but its victim as well. With Rimbaud, poetry became a language deformed wilfully, an instrument turning in all directions like a surgical knife, the cancerous question: of what is man capable? with what is formed the vision of man? Art exists in its rigid ultimate form but the human intelligence which first conceived it continues living, either seeing more clearly into man's destiny or seeing more darkly into a pyrrhonic philosophy.

In Rimbaud's poetry we can experience a delectation in our approximate understanding of his vision (and this is all art seeks to do; namely, to cause delight in the contemplation of its beauty). But Rimbaud's experience which caused his poetry to come into existence, continued in mystery and silence after his creative instinct was arrested, and this experience will always be incomprehensible to our minds. Rimbaud understood that he didn't understand. This might have been subject enough for a poet's art. It was, in Baudelaire's case, who modeled and strengthened the "idea," at times with irony, at times with tenderness. But with Rimbaud there was but one treatment of darkness, its quality of black, and it ended by stifling him.

Baudelaire was the artist of despair because he coped with it in his art. Rimbaud was its victim because as an artist he abandoned it. Both Baudelaire and Rimbaud prepared the advent of Claudel who accepts the world as an obstacle to be conquered, as a bestower of dignity, as a means to an end ineffable. The majesty of the great: Dante, Shakespeare, Claudel, seems to derive from their participation in the world, from their love of the world, a love warmed by pity and a sense of unrealized heritage. Every page of Claudel is pervaded with the belief that what is born from a chisel or from a pen is destined to the multiple deaths of the grass and the sun. What is common to Dante, to Shakespeare, to Claudel is the primacy of man's spiritual problem. Their art is opacity of sounds and transparency of ideas. In their art is subsumed the unity belonging to man. Man insufficient and beguiled, yet capable of joy in wisdom. The art of Dante and Shakespeare depicts the manifold stages of man's despair and joy. The art of Dante and Claudel speaks of the visitation of what is called Grace, the repairer of maimed humanity.

To experience an art one must enter a climate of darkness or a climate of grace. To understand an art one must be initiated to the smile of the infant Jesus playing with a pomegranate or to the sombre destiny of a Dostoievsky character. For the spectator, in both cases, it is a question of succumbing. For the artist, in both cases, it is a question of reproducing the clear part of obscurity.

To continue and to conclude what resembles a geometrical progression:—if Baudelaire is the artist of darkness and Rimbaud its victim, and if Claudel is the artist of light, there is a type of artist we can consider the victim of light. He is the contemplative, a St. John of the Cross or a St. Theresa. We have been concerned with the kind of man who reaches toward the inaccessible, toward the formless. In the composing of his poetry, the poet doesn't relinquish any part of his human nature. The delectation which we experience intellectually in the presence of art trains and prepares us for contemplation, which from the Thomistic viewpoint is the greatest of delectations. The creation of art represents a moment in man's search for the unity which the mystic apprehends in contemplation and which Plotinus describes as an accordance with partlessness. The artist sees the things of this realm; the mystic uses them as a point of departure in order to see.

In this very broad view of the validity of man's spiritual experience, the artist's activity is only an initial stage, a prefiguration of a subsequent and greater one. If the mystic attains the ultimate delectation, art is impoverishing and contemplation is fecundating.

Man lives only in the marvellous ubiquity of his hopes. His glance is vertiginous and his heart dishabituates itself of the present. The first difficult lesson is to learn what is truly ourselves. And then we must learn that nature and man disappear or change. We must first awaken to the perpetual flow of everything in order to arrive at the vision of that which is not measured by time.

Poetry's province is the unknowing fluidity of days. The mobility of the skies is in poetry. The immobility of heaven is not in poetry.

NOTES

1. *The acrobats* of Picasso epitomize the frailty of our age and the spiritual hope in something as yet unrealized. They represent both the period and its legend. They have lived through two wars telling us uninterruptedly that no war is ever ended. The deep sea divers of Cocteau's poetry also repeated on their white pages that this age is enacted in a dream, that both its order and its disorder spring from dilemmas.

Again, it is France that speaks. The French artists and those who, like Picasso, have profoundly undergone the lesson of France, have insisted on describing what they see and not what the world sees. France in the twentieth, as in the seventeenth century, is the sole land where there is an agreement between man and life.

2. The failure of all this generation is the failure to distinguish between good and evil. Man cannot remain inert and speechless when he feels this conflict in himself and sees it act in the world. Whether it be "action" in drama or "desire" in living, the two spheres of good and evil are ever present: light and darkness of all creation; the counterparts and antipodes of man's word.

God said to Isaiah, "I form the light, and create darkness." (*Formans lucem et creans tenebras.*)

The history of man could be written in accordance with the cycles of his knowledge about good and evil and of his ignorance about them. In this century, the germs of thought, sown in the Renaissance, have fully matured and their flowering has obscured the Middle Ages. We are in the process of becoming again children, but we shall not have the innocency of children. "They have not known nor understood: for he hath shut their eyes, that they cannot see; and their hearts, that they cannot understand."

3. It would be false to say that the inner struggle of the modern hero has lost all the aspects of the ancient hero's struggle to realize

155

himself and to accept the good. The modern seeks to make real what is unreal and to create a new self freed from all the strictures of the original self. Michel and Stephen do not think of grace as the repairer of the human soul. If they did consider grace, they would have probably feared that it destroys the obstacles it meets in a soul. Hamlet knew that grace uses all the obstacles it meets.

4. Gide the artist does not essentially resemble Proust the artist who seeks the satisfaction of love recreated in its most minute suffering. Rather, Gide is the writer who seeks the grace of any act, of any inclination, the freshness of every moment as it is lived. This word "moment" is an important one for both Proust and Gide. Proust's work is the artistic forgery of a moment (or a series of moments) that had been lived—the moment weighted down by the years which had followed it. But Gide's moment, as it is transcribed in his books, bears the buoyancy and the unexpectedness of its initial experience. Time is not then for Gide what it was for Proust: the process of memory growing and fecundating itself; it is the chemistry which annihilates memory and responsibility, the force which truncates the past and makes gloriously autonomous the present.

5. The apparitions of Charlus throughout the long work of Proust form a major theme which is in some respects comparable to the theme of Swann's love. At first, this theme appears inconspicuously. He is the man who abruptly changes his attitude toward people. At each appearance the theme is more developed and continues to grow in importance until, at the end of the work, he occupies a dominant place and is the central figure in elaborate episodes. Does this mean that Charlus undergoes in the book an evolution of his own? I think not. Charlus is simply the character whom one heeds more and more. Even during his early brief appearances, his character is completely delineated in the reduced notations of Proust which are very much like the first hearing of a theme in a long composition. After the first reading of the novel (and Proust is not the author to read for the first time), Charlus appears complete in the slightest of his gestures. When Mme. de Villeparisis introduces Marcel to the baron, the latter heeds the boy very little and continues to look intensely at some insignificant strangers. (*A l'Ombre des*

Jeunes Filles en Fleurs, 2, p. 211.) This activity of Charlus' penetrating eyes is his first theme. He is the man watching, a kind of poacher watching silently for prey. He is the man who watches in silence and who will recognize when the time comes, because he is the man who has determined his fate.

In order to be heroic, one must not know one's fate, one must undergo it. The character of Charlus determines the work of his creator, as sickness had determined the life of Proust. Charlus is the man who invents his life and buys. He will never sell it as most men have to sell theirs. Around him and thanks to him, the literary work takes on its substance and grows, from the first faint announcement of his theme to the final full development of his scenes. In Charlus every trace of the innocent hero has disappeared. He is the monster who watches life knowingly from the dark room of his desires and experiences.

The peremptory tone of Charlus and his haughtiness of attitude in conversations are traits as characteristic of him as quiet aloofness and aesthetic passion are characteristic of Swann. Both heroes are close to one another in their belief that the important thing in life is to love. (cf. *Jeunes Filles*, 2, p. 224.) Whereas Swann loves the woman who is different from him, Charlus is going to fall in love with those whom society forbids him to love. His passion is the passion of Andromaque and Phèdre. He discovers the truth of passion in what is monstrous and abnormal, and because of this very monstrosity the passion of love in Charlus glows more clearly than in ordinary love. He himself refers to the love of Mme. de Sévigné for her daughter and compares the superficial treatment of love in Hugo's dramas with the fierceness of love in Racine's tragedies. Charlus, seduced by the youth of Marcel on the beach at Balbec, plays the tragic scene of love without words and without hope. His fate, as was Swann's to a considerable degree, is that of a man attracted toward those who will never understand him.

6. The theme of Paris in the poetry of Villon and Baudelaire offers an example of a fundamental difference between mediaeval and modern art, between the universality of mediaeval Christian art and the individualism of modern Christian poetry.

No poet as much as Villon, if it isn't Baudelaire, is so completely the spiritual offspring of Paris. Nature plays no part in his poetic work, but the spectacle of Paris is everywhere. The gossiping tongues of fishwives and the salacious oaths of cut-throats and the incense of Notre Dame are all parts of the city's lyricism. Villon's nature is that of the Parisian plebeian who has no face to berouge. He is the son of the city that demands of its writers wit as well as genius, the first of a company which will count among its members a Molière, a Beaumarchais, a Voltaire.

The depth of humanity that Villon reached is the miracle of his poetry. Although his work is totally localized, it has universality because it is the work of a man and not of an author. There is an absence of any conversion, but there is also an absence of any hypocrisy. It is the poetry of a man who, because he is about to die, has the right to say anything.

The history of Villon is that of a bad boy, a cynic, a mediaeval gangster. The poetry of Villon is that of a man who sees himself as the most imperfect of God's creatures, who resists God and yet who can conceive the hope that the gates of Paradise will be opened to him. He exemplifies the moral tone of the Middle Ages by his belief that there is no sinner so lost that he cannot be saved. In supplicating the Virgin for mercy, he was doing what the whole Middle Ages did. He was accepting the lesson of the Church which announces that the reign of equality takes place after the tomb.

These are the reasons why Villon's art can be called a Christian art. Although far removed from the art of Dante and Fra Angelico, it is as Christian as theirs because it is the art of a humanity conscious of its redemption. The more a man becomes capable of remorse, the greater a Christian he is. Living for Villon became the crime, but his conscience expiated it. Perpetual despair was the law of Villon's life. He was a Christian first in realizing that this despair was engendered by crime and secondly, in realizing that there was above him a Justice. He knew also that this Justice would not smile upon him through any birthrights. Only through the exercise of moral will would his soul enjoy serenity.

7. Villon, in reflecting so poignantly man's inner struggle between good and evil, follows the cadence of the Middle Ages, and particularly that of his own century, when antitheses of every nature were

more apparent than in other periods. It was a time when great devotion to the Virgin was manifested and it was a time celebrated for bandits and plunderers. It produced a Joan of Arc and a Gilles de Rais. Louis XI took delight in torturing his captives and in collecting religious relics. On Saturdays the students left their various schools on the Montagne Sainte Geneviève and used to pray in large groups before the statue of the Virgin in Notre Dame. But afterwards, they would pay a visit to the prostitutes who lived in close proximity to the cathedral. The same crowds that watched public executions with excitement, attended reverently the mystery plays. Villon was only six when Charles VII entered Paris and gave the city an impressive festivity. This was followed by an epidemic that killed fifty thousand people.

8. Beyond the fact that she was a pious parishioner of a convent church ornamented with a fresco depicting hell and paradise, nothing is known of Villon's mother. Yet through the miracle of a few verses the world remembers her devotion to Our Lady. Almost accidently Villon reveals the great reality of her character: her tender piety, her indestructible faith which influenced her son and to which he owes some of the loftiest moments of his life. When Villon refers to her in his poetry, he calls her a castle and a fortress where he may shelter his body and soul:

> "Autre chastel n'ay, ne forteresse,
> Ou me retraye corps et ame."

9. Villon's art partakes of a quality inherent in all mediaeval art, a quality almost inaccessible to modern sensibility. The cathedrals, the Gregorian plainsong, mediaeval lyric poetry are not so much the expression of artists as they are the expression of an entire race, a race which had one religion, one philosophy, one language. Art was for the people. They lived in its presence without realizing it was beauty. St. Thomas taught that beauty is that which gives joy and that beauty is of an intellectual order. The artist is the intellectual who operates and his virtue is the virtue of the intelligence. It is impossible to say that the despair in Villon's art is comparable to the despair of a modern, because Villon understood so clearly his despair. The themes in Villon's poetry had been treated before him; the structure of his

testaments was a legacy from the period of Latin decadence. His poetry contains more pathos and more artistic finish, but it is nevertheless the mirror of the conscience of his entire race.

10. Racine not only completes his age; he surpasses it. With the force of a whole nation supporting him, he is the artist who remains superior to his work. What a contrasting fate with that of Villon, whose work is the pathetic confession of his life; and with that of Dante, whose work is lesson and reproval to a world which had banished him and which he still loved.

The plays of Racine are not the literary expression of his life; in fact they are not faithful to life itself. Their strange miracle is that they transmit the sombre horrors of life without in any way imitating life.

11. Villon often speaks directly to himself, but his poetry is peopled with countless characters from every class and every age. Vices and virtues appear side by side. Their commingling in this single voice which echoes so many voices stresses the spirit of coherence and universality characteristic of the Middle Ages. The work thus takes its place beside the Sainte Chapelle, the *Divine Comedy* and the *Summa* of St. Thomas, first because it is an artistic achievement in harmony with the period, and secondly because the artist is striving for something beyond his work and because the work is subordinate to the destiny of man and human virtues.

INDEX

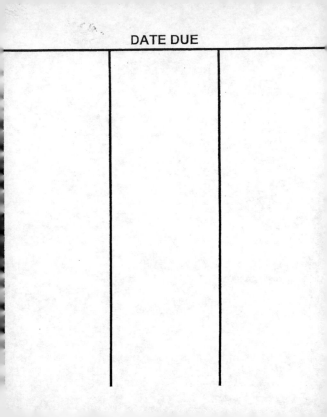

DATE DUE